ALSO BY DAVID OWEN

High School

None of the Above

The Man Who Invented Saturday Morning

The Walls Around Us

My Usual Game

Around the House
(also published as *Life Under a Leaky Roof*)

Lure of the Links (co-editor)

The Making of the Masters

The Complete Office Golf

The Chosen One

Hit & Hope

Copies in Seconds

Sheetrock & Shellac

THE FIRST NATIONAL
Bank *of* DAD

A Foolproof Method for
Teaching Your Kids the Value of Money

DAVID OWEN

SIMON & SCHUSTER PAPERBACKS
NEW YORK   LONDON   TORONTO   SYDNEY

Simon & Schuster Paperbacks
Rockefeller Center
1230 Avenue of the Americas
New York, NY 10020

SIMON & SCHUSTER PAPERBACKS and colophon are
registered trademarks of Simon & Schuster, Inc.

For information about special discounts for bulk purchases,
please contact Simon & Schuster Special Sales:
at 1-800-456-6798 or business@simonandschuster.com

Designed by Jan Pisciotta

Manufactured in the United States of America

10 9 8 7 6 5 4 3 2 1

The Library of Congress has cataloged the hardcover edition as follows:
Owen, David, 1955–
The first national bank of dad : the best way to teach kids
about money / David Owen.
p.   cm.
1. Children—Finance, Personal. I. Title.
HG179.0876 2003
332.024'054—dc21   2002026675

ISBN-13: 978-0-7432-0480-4
ISBN-10:   0-7432-0480-8
ISBN-13: 978-1-4165-3425-9 (Pbk)
ISBN-10:   1-4165-3425-3 (Pbk)

For my father

Contents

THE FIRST NATIONAL
Bank *of* DAD

1

CHILDREN AND MONEY: AN INTRODUCTION

WHEN OUR SON WAS BORN, my wife and I needed a baby blanket for his crib. Our daughter, who was three and a half, had several old ones in her closet.

"What are you doing in my closet?" she demanded.

"Just getting one of these old blankets," my wife said.

"Why?"

"To give it to your new baby brother."

"I want it!" our daughter screamed.

"But, honey," I said, "you didn't even know that old blanket was there."

"I need it!"

"It's a *baby* blanket. Don't you want to give it to a *baby*?"

"I want it!"

My wife and I looked at each other in despair. What to do? Suddenly, my wife had an inspiration.

"Would you take five bucks for it?" she asked.

(No more crying.) "O.K."

Money is a handy tool if you use it wisely. Even very young children get the hang of it in a hurry. In the baby-blanket incident just described, my wife narrowly averted a family crisis by offering to swap an emotionally neutral symbol (money) for an emotionally loaded one (the old blanket). With a crisp five-dollar bill in her piggy bank, our daughter felt justly compensated for this latest unpleasant ramification of the birth of her baby brother. And my wife and I were delighted to give her the cash, because doing so let us go back to what we had been doing before the argument arose: changing diapers, ignoring laundry, and not getting enough sleep.*

If my wife hadn't suddenly thought of monetary compensation, our fight would have escalated along a predictable trajectory: my wife and I would have stepped up our efforts to make our daughter feel like a bad child, and our daughter would have stepped up her efforts to

---

*With similar ingenuity, my wife once solved the age-old problem of how to keep young children from bickering while walking single file. She did it by creating the position of "back leader," thereby making both ends of a line seem important. Occasionally, she designated a "middle leader" as well.

make us feel like bad parents. Instead, everyone went to bed that night in a pretty good mood. A couple of months later, our daughter even reconciled herself to the idea of no longer being an only child. Walking alongside her brother's stroller, she said suddenly, with a sigh of resignation, "I don't know who I'll marry. *Him, I guess.*"

GROWN-UPS ARE DUMB

Money is so easy to understand in theory that you'd think more people would do a good job of handling it in practice. But they don't. In many families, financial matters become a psychological theater of war not only between parents and children but also between parents and parents. Why does that happen? We probably don't want to know the real reasons. (One family's story: I claim to think money is pure pragmatism, while my wife believes it's all symbolism and neurosis.) But there are ways of sidestepping the problem altogether, especially where children are concerned—as long as parents take advantage of human nature instead of ignoring it or futilely attempting to change it.

Most efforts by most parents to teach most kids about money are doomed from the start. Those efforts usually begin (and often end) with the opening of savings accounts. The parents suddenly decide that the time has come to impose order on their children's chaotic financial affairs, so they march the kids down to the bank and sign them up for passbooks. The children are intrigued at first by the notion that a bank will pay them for doing nothing, but their enthusiasm fades when they realize that the interest rate is minuscule and, furthermore, that their parents don't intend to give them access to their principal. To a kid, a savings account is just a black hole that swallows birthday checks.

Kid: "Grandma gave me twenty-five dollars!"

Parent: "How nice. We'll put that check straight into your savings account."

Kid: "But she gave it to me! I want it!"

Parent: "Oh, it will still be yours. You just have to keep it in the bank so that it can grow."

Kid (suspicious): "What do you mean 'grow'?"

Parent: "Well, if you leave your twenty-five dollars in the bank for just one year, the bank will pay you *fifty cents.* And if you leave all of *that* in the bank for just one *more* year, the bank will give you another fifty cents, plus an extra penny besides. That's called compound interest. It will help you go to college."

The main problem with these schemes is that there's nothing in them for the kids. College seems a thousand years away to young children—who, at this point, probably think they'd just as soon stay home, anyway—and the promised annual return wouldn't cover even the cost of a pack of chewing gum. Most children immediately realize that banking plans implemented by their parents are actually punitive in intent: their true purpose is not to promote saving but to prevent consumption. Appalled by what their children spend on candy and video games—and also appalled, perhaps, by the degree to which their children's profligacy seems to mimic their own—the parents devise stratagems for impounding excess resources.

Almost every family has its unspoken point of no return—a limit above which monetary gifts are considered too large to be entrusted to young spenders. According to the perverse arithmetic that parents thus impose, a five-dollar bill (which a child is usually allowed to keep) is far more valuable to the child than a hundred-dollar check (which parents usually expropriate and "save"). Not surprisingly, kids soon decide that large sums aren't real money and that all cash should either be spent immediately or hidden in a drawer.

I know these things happen, because I made all the same mistakes. When my daughter reached kindergarten, I gave her a lecture on the virtues of fiscal prudence, then opened a savings account in her name with a deposit of a hundred dollars. Her excitement about my scheme, never great, sank to zero when I told her that she would not be allowed to touch that money any time soon. No matter how enthusiastically I praised the American banking system, she viewed her savings account as a fiction.

My first reaction was that she must be too young, or maybe too lazy, to plan, in a mature and responsible fashion, for her old age. However, on further reflection (over the course of several years, unfortunately), I realized that the problem wasn't a defect in her character; the problem was a defect in my plan. After all, I don't have a savings account myself—and why should I? I'd rather keep money in a mattress than do all that driving back and forth to the bank for a lousy 2 percent per annum. I store my wealth in the same places you store yours: in stocks and bonds and real estate and money-market accounts and other investments, all of which generate better returns over time than a dumb old savings account.* Why had I believed that a five-year-old, for whom a year seems to last at least a decade, would be impressed by handfuls of pennies doled out over eons? Hadn't I closed out my own childhood savings account the moment it came under my sole control? (Yes.)

I had also forgotten that, to a kid, "long term" does

*In recent years, passbook interest rates haven't looked as bad as they used to. Over long periods of time, though, passbook interest rates are just about the lowest of the low.

not mean "long term"—it means "never." Encouraging a nursery-schooler to save for college is like encouraging a fifty-year-old to save for the colonization of Mars. When I was five, a century did not seem longer to me than the period between my first day of kindergarten and the day when I would finally be old enough to do the one thing I wanted to do more than anything in life: drive a car. (A further proof, as if any were needed, that time passes more slowly for children than it does for adults: you never hear a grown-up say, "I'm six hundred and seventy-three months old"—although I did once hear a forty-year-old say, "I'm half-dead now.")

This perception of the passage of time isn't even an illusion where children are concerned; when parents talk to their kids about "long term" in connection with money, the parents usually do mean "never." Parents force their children to lock away their money because the parents hate to think what their children would do with that money if they could. The real purpose of almost all parent-mandated saving schemes is not self-improvement but confiscation. A savings account is just a jail in which parents incarcerate their children's money so that their children's money won't be able to go around causing trouble when the parents aren't looking.

REAL REASONS TO SAVE

You and I don't think of saving for ourselves as a form of punishment. You and I save because we are convinced that saving will make our lives better, and that it will do so while we are still on hand to enjoy the fun. If we sacrifice some spending now, we believe, then someday in the foreseeable future we will be able to buy a fancier car, or play more golf, or add a swimming pool to our yard, or send our kids to more impressive-sounding colleges, or retire at eighty-five instead of ninety. In other words, we save for selfish reasons. We spend less money now in order to spend more money later.

If children are to become savers, I suddenly realized, then they need selfish reasons, too—selfish reasons that make sense to them. To be attractive to a child, saving has to make life better for the child—and the benefits have to be tangible, just as they are for adults. Those benefits also have to arrive in what to the child seems like real time, rather than being pushed so far into the future that in the mind of the child they simply do not exist.

Most important of all, I realized that up until that moment almost all of my efforts to teach my daughter financial responsibility had consisted of reducing or eliminating what few financial responsibilities she had. How could she possibly learn anything about handling money if I was just going to keep dreaming up new excuses for taking money out of her hands? Don't we learn about money the way we learn about anything else—by making a series of gradually less horrible mistakes and living with the consequences?

I think we do. And it was all of these realizations that led to the ideas that I describe in the rest of this book.

GOOD OLD SHORTCUTS

Of course, the notion of setting out to teach children about money is nutty, in a sense, because all of us parents have been teaching our children about money on a daily basis ever since they became old enough to notice the difference between them and us. We teach them about money every time we make a wise or foolish purchase, brag or weep about a recent experience in the stock market, appear happy or sad when we return home from work, capitulate or fail to capitulate when they focus their energies on persuading us to buy them something idiotic, and either pay off our credit cards or run up our debts to the point where we prefer to let an answering machine handle our incoming calls. Over the course of an entire childhood, these mostly unconscious lessons make a deeper impression on our kids than anything we might think to tell them. The best way to teach a child about money, therefore, is to live a life in which money plays just the right role, whatever that is, and to set nothing but good examples, whatever those are.*

Holy cow, though, that's a depressing thought. For one thing, setting good examples is exhausting. For another thing, I, like most parents, want to shape my children directly, through the application of powerful child-rearing techniques. I don't want to sit back and let nature take its dreary course; I want to use scientific methods to program my offspring to surpass my own meager accomplishments in life and to build large personal fortunes with which they will be able to sustain my wife and me in our old age. And I want to do it quickly and easily, without having to turn myself into a better person.

Shortcuts, then. As luck would have it, there are some good ones.

---

*Alternatively, we can set nothing but terrible examples, and hope that by doing so we will leave our children no choice but to rebel against us, enabling them to find happiness by rejecting everything we stand for.

SOME ADVICE ABOUT ADVICE

Before I get to that, though, I want to deal with a couple of preliminary issues. First, I want to answer a question that I suspect may be forming in the minds of some readers: Does teaching children about money turn them into money-grubbing creeps?

My answer is, No, of course not—as long as what we teach them is rational. In fact, one of the goals of teaching children about money is to prevent them from ever becoming money-grubbing creeps. The more thoroughly children understand money—and the more comfortable they feel in its presence—the less likely they will be to become obsessed or overwhelmed by it as they get older.

I'm not one of these people who claim that greed is good. Greed is very bad indeed, because it is insatiable and because it, like all addictions, leads only to unhappiness. One of the goals of teaching children about money is to make them immune to greed, by helping them learn to view money intelligently and unemotionally, as a practical tool for improving their lives.

I had a friend in college who decided, in a typical gesture of adolescent absolutism, to stop wearing a wristwatch. He was tired of being hung up about time, man, so he freed himself from civilization's arbitrary and oppressive chronological prison. The joke, of course, is that without a watch he was forced to think about time all the time. Soon, he was spending a large part of every day asking other people what time it was—a necessity, since his professors and the operators of local movie theaters, among others, still paid attention to the clock. Getting rid of his watch didn't liberate him; it turned him into a raving timeaholic.

Children should learn about money for the same reason that my friend soon went back to wearing a watch: to keep them from having to devote too much determined mental energy to an activity that often works better at the level of reflex. One learns about money partly in order to stop brooding about it. And no one spends more time brooding about money than someone who is scared of it, or who doesn't understand it, or who willfully tries to ignore it.

The other issue I want to address has to do with advice. Almost all the advice books I've ever read have followed one or the other of two basic pedagogical strategies: they have either taken something virtually impossible and made it sound pretty easy (losing weight, becoming physically fit), or taken something pretty easy and made it sound virtually impossible (raising children who aren't totally screwed up).

Financial advice usually conforms to the first model. As you read some expert's ten surefire rules for achieving financial freedom, you think, "Gee, I'd have to be a moron not to be rich by the time I close this book." Then, of course, reality sets in—and the stocks you buy go down instead of up, and you can't find a supplier who is willing to sell you deeply discounted rolls of commercial-grade toilet paper by the gross, and no bank seems eager to offer you an unsecured ten-million-dollar loan so that you can renovate the abandoned apartment building that you are planning to buy in a foreclosure auction with no money down. If advice books really worked as well as they claim to, there wouldn't be so many of them. One how-to-take-off-fifteen-pounds-and-keep-them-off guide would be plenty for everyone, thank you, and we would never outgrow our clothes.

In addition, I suspect that most of us think that reading or listening to good advice is a perfectly acceptable substitute for following it. I know I feel that way about *Consumer Reports,* which I have read faithfully for many years. I love that magazine's careful analyses of various consumer products, but I'm pretty sure that I have never actually made a purchase based on any of the articles. What I tend to do is buy first and then—days, weeks, or months later—discover in the magazine whether my purchase was sensible or not. Subscribing to *Consumer Reports* makes me feel like a smart shopper, but consistently following its advice would be an awful lot of trouble. In fact, I'd be willing to bet that even the people who test products for Consumers Union probably feel largely the way I do, and that their homes are filled with stuff that didn't do all that well when they evaluated it for *Consumer Reports.*

Another confession: I myself don't always follow all of the advice in this book. No one could. (I also would guess that Jane Brody, the "Personal Health" columnist of the *New York Times,* hasn't put wide strips of reflective tape on the risers of her stairs, as she once advised her readers to do.) Real life is too complicated to be conducted sensibly at all times, and all of us are not only different but also busy. I think I've done a good job of helping my kids develop reasonably healthy attitudes about money, but we've had our moments, believe me.

The goal is to raise children who aren't overwhelmed by the financial side of life, and there is more than one way to achieve that goal. You can pick and choose among my ideas, or you can be inspired to cook up ideas of your own, or you can leave the whole thing alone and hope for the best. My own kids' interest in financial matters has ebbed and flowed over the years, and it has been heavily influenced at times by such seemingly extraneous matters as how much homework they had that night and who was going to the mall.

Besides, no one's life should be dominated by what someone else thinks about money, even if what someone else thinks about money is awfully smart.

2

THE FIRST NATIONAL BANK OF DAD

IF YOU AND A YOUNG CHILD ever find yourselves with time on your hands—somewhere toward the middle of a long car trip, say—you may be able to keep the two of you amused for a little while by explaining the concept of compound interest. Start by asking the child if he or she would like to earn some extra spending money. If the child says yes, say something like the following:

"I've got a chore that might appeal to you. I'm tired of taking care of our dogs all by myself, and I'm willing to pay you or someone else to help me. What I want is somebody to feed the dogs every morning and every night, and change their water once a day, and take them for a walk four times a day, and bathe them once a week. For all of that, I would be willing to pay one cent a day.

If you do a good job the first day, I'll double the pay to two cents the second day. If you do a good job the second day, I'll double the pay again, to four cents, on the third day, and so on, doubling every day, as long as you keep doing a good job. What do you think?"

"You're out of your mind!" the child would scream.

At least, you should hope the child would scream that. Here's why: a wage that began at a penny a day and doubled every day thereafter would hit more than five million dollars in thirty days, and from there it would take off for the stars.*

CHILD-SIZED RATES OF RETURN

If bank balances doubled every day, we would have no trouble making kids feel excited about savings accounts. Heck, I'd open one myself. There's just one problem: the world would run out of money so fast that the lesson wouldn't have time to sink in. To double every day, a

---

*If you try this on a child and the child takes you up on your offer, don't panic. Let the child look after the dogs for a week at the agreed-upon rate. Then say, in a tone of deep disappointment, "Per our original agreement, your continued employment by me is contingent upon your satisfactory performance of the stipulated duties. I'm sorry to say that you have ceased to fulfill that requirement. You're fired." Whew!

bank account would have to offer an annual rate of return of 3,757,668,132,438,133,164,623,168,954,862, 939,243,801,092,078,253,311,793,131,665,554,451,534, 440,183,373,509,541,918,397,415,629,924,851,095,961, 500 percent. (That's the real rate, incidentally; it was calculated for me by a friend who had access to a mainframe computer owned by a large multinational corporation.)

The only difference, mathematically, between a bank account that doubles every day and a regular passbook savings account is time. Doubling has exactly the same miraculous effect in both instances, but in the passbook savings account each doubling takes an excruciatingly long time to occur. In fact, with a passbook account that pays interest at a rate of 2 percent per year, turning that first penny into two pennies would require a bit more than thirty-five years, and turning it into five million dollars would require roughly a millennium.

It was while thinking about this phenomenon—which is also known as exponential growth—that I suddenly realized what I needed to do to make my children become interested in saving: I needed to offer them a rate of return that would seem exciting to them, and would make them decide voluntarily that saving was a good idea. That rate of return wouldn't have to be (and obviously couldn't be) 100 percent a day. But it would definitely have to be higher than any bank's regular passbook rate. After a lot of thought, I decided that the rate would have to be high enough to provide a child with indisputable evidence of real growth in just one month—an interval that probably represents the maximum realistic long-term time horizon for a six-year-old. I also decided that the rate would have to be high enough to make the miracle of compounding obvious to the child, by causing deposits to double in value in not much more than a year.

I knew that no commercial bank would offer a sufficiently attractive rate, so I decided to open a bank of my own. I called it the First National Bank of Dad, and I invited my children to become my first (and only) depositors. I told them that I wanted to encourage them to save some of their money instead of spending it all right away, and I said that I was pretty sure that I had thought of a way to do that. If they would agree to keep some of their money in my bank, I said, I would pay them interest on their balances at the rate of 5 percent per month. That's right—per month. Compounded monthly, that works out to an annual rate of more than 70 percent, and a doubling interval of approximately fifteen months. (No, I don't accept deposits from adults or from children who didn't receive half of their chromosomes from me.) "If you hang on to some of your wealth," I told them, "in a little while, you'll be able to double or even triple your allowance. The more you save, and the longer you hold it, the more you will be able to spend."

LETTING MONEY "CHARGE UP"

Neither of my kids—who were six and ten at the time—really understood what an interest rate was, but they both instantly grasped the idea. I started them off with a balance of twenty-five dollars apiece, and I told them that if they left that sum in my bank all month, they'd earn an extra buck and a quarter, over and above their allowances. What's more, I said, the following month they would earn interest on the whole pile, and they could add additional money (or take out money) at any time. I told them I would credit their interest on the last day of every month and their allowances on the first. (For a discussion of allowances, see Chapter 4.) My son, impatient to boost his income from the outset, searched our cars and all our upholstered furniture for change, turning up several dollars' worth. "And credit this today," he said as he dumped it on my desk.

My kids had never been savers before. Both had been accustomed to spending all their money as soon as they got their hands on it—undoubtedly because they were worried that my wife or I would suddenly think of a reason to snatch it from them if they didn't. When the kids received money as a gift from a relative, for example, their usual reaction had been to ask to be driven to the mall that very day, so that they could immediately convert their cash into finished goods, which are harder for grown-ups to seize.

But the Bank of Dad changed their attitude. With their accounts in place, the kids would hand all their windfalls over to me the moment they received them, so that their idle cash could start racking up interest as soon as possible. A few months after I opened for business, my son explained his new financial philosophy. Instead of spending his cash right away, he told me, he now liked to let his money "charge up" for a while before letting some of it go. In school a year or two later, he explored the same concept in a science-fiction story: "If I had one million dollars," he wrote,

> I would put it in the bank. Then I would make
> a good tasting grape potion that would make
> me live much longer. Then in 10281 I would
> take my money out of the bank and instead of
> 1 million dollars I would have
> $100000000000,0000000000000!

In an accompanying illustration, he depicted himself concocting his life-extending potion (from grape soda and ice), while a fleet of armored cars, in the background, transported his refulgent fortune to his mansion.

BECOMING RICH

Within a couple of years of the founding of the Bank of Dad, both of my kids had methodically built their balances to the point where their monthly income (allowance plus interest and gifts) exceeded their monthly expenses by a comfortable margin. They were then able to keep themselves well supplied with comic books, music, candy, and other day-to-day necessities while continuing to build their nest eggs for the future. In time, each child had enough money in reserve to cover a reasonably extravagant purchase without unduly diminishing his or her principal. But they felt no anxious pressure to make those acquisitions. Because they knew their money belonged to them—and because they knew that it was working for them in the background—they didn't feel compelled to spend it rashly.

In other words, they treated their money the way sensible grown-ups have always claimed that money ought to be treated. And they did it without my haranguing them about the virtues of restraint. As soon as their savings began to grow at a rate that was meaningful to them, they realized that frenzied spending was not in their best interest.

The moral is that money is beautifully self-explanatory—as long as you let it do the talking.

Permit Me to Repeat Myself

This point is so important that it is worth making a second time: Your children already have a pretty good idea of how money works. That's why they've never been excited about your compulsory savings-account schemes. To turn them into savers, you don't need to change the way they think about money; you just need to offer them a truly attractive option that lets their money work for them in the same way your money works for you. Human nature, that irresistible force, will take things from there. The Bank of Dad turned my children into savers because it gave them, for the first time in their lives, a real incentive to save. If they deferred consumption for a while, they realized, they would eventually be able to consume more.

That is exactly why grown-ups save. The lesson to be drawn from my kids' experience is that children will save all by themselves—without coercion or tedious moralizing from adults—as long as their money is allowed to grow fast enough for them to notice the effect. All we have to do to turn our children into savers is to give them an incentive that seems like an incentive *to them*. The meager returns that satisfy beaten-down, mortality-fearing adults won't do, because at those rates money accumulates far too slowly to dent their awareness.

I took several economics courses during my freshman and sophomore years in college. The subject excited me from the start, because basic free-market economics seemed to provide an extraordinarily compact explanation for a huge range of human behavior: people tend to do what they are rewarded for doing. If you want to change people's behavior (economics teaches us), berating, cajoling, and pleading work less well than adjusting the incentives. That's why the United States is still around and the Soviet Union isn't. My kids did not become savers because I restricted their spending or lectured them about the immorality of profligacy or preached to them about the virtues of thrift. They became savers because I created a system that rewarded them for spending less than they earned.

How to Build a Bank of Your Own

Actually establishing the Bank of Dad was easy—I did it on my personal computer. With help from my kids, I set up a checking account for each of them in Quicken, the financial software I use to keep track of my own spending. The program didn't know and didn't care that these accounts were fictitious, in the sense that they didn't reside in an actual bank with actual tellers and an actual vault. Quicken treated the accounts as though they were real, and so did my kids and I.

I configured Quicken to add the children's allowances automatically on the first day of every month—a simple procedure, which I use in my own (real) checking account to deduct my automatic monthly payment for health insurance. I had hoped, initially, that Quicken would also be able to automatically calculate and add the interest I intended to pay on the kids' accounts, but I couldn't figure out how to make the software do that, if it even can. So I did my interest calculations manually and entered the information myself.

A personal computer is a handy accessory for anyone operating a bank for children, but it isn't a necessity. All the record-keeping that I did electronically could also be done in a paper-check register or, for that matter, on a sheet of plain paper. One great advantage of using a computer program, though, is that the program simplifies the recording of transactions out of sequence, so that you can go back and fill in a few forgotten interest payments, let's say, without then being forced to erase and recalculate everything that follows. Computerized banking programs also handle all the math automatically, so that you are no longer forced to submit yourself to the humiliation of incorrectly adding and subtracting elementary sums. (I used Quicken, but there are other programs that would work just as well, including Microsoft Money. You could also keep track of children's accounts in a simple spreadsheet, or in a table that you created in a word-processing program.)

My kids were extremely excited about the Bank of Dad when I first explained the idea to them. They made business cards and a sign for me, and we used a desktop publishing program and a color ink-jet printer to create some shockingly real-looking checks. My original idea was that whenever the kids needed cash, they would write a check in that amount to my wife or me, and we would hand over the cash; then I would "clear" the checks by posting them in Quicken.

As things turned out, though, dealing all that paper began to seem like a hassle after just a few days, and from that point forward we abandoned the checks and allowed the bank to operate more or less on the honor system. The kids would ask for money when they wanted it, and my wife or I would give it to them and make a note of the amount (assuming that their balances were sufficient to cover the withdrawals), and then at some point I would bring things up to date on my computer. Occasionally, I would realize that a couple of now semi-forgotten transactions had accidentally gone unrecorded, so I would make a balance adjustment in what seemed to me to be a fair amount. We all agreed that these haphazard accounting procedures were unavoidable, given the nature of the depositors, the banker, and the bank. And any errors were small and tended to even out over time.

A Cash Machine in the Kitchen

If my kids and I were starting all over again right now with the Bank of Dad, I might further simplify the money-handling by creating a family cash machine. I would put a hundred dollars' worth of five- and ten-dollar bills in a box in the kitchen, and I would tell the kids to make their own withdrawals and deposits and to record the date, nature, and amount of each transaction on a piece of paper inside the box. I would maintain the cash supply and periodically update the records on my computer.

An arrangement like that wouldn't work with larcenous children, of course. But if you have two or more children and they are semi-dependable, you can make such a system virtually self-regulating by telling the children that any shortfalls in the cash box will be charged equally and in full against the accounts of all depositors. That will make your children fight with one another instead of whining or lying to you. (I borrowed that idea from Clifford Roberts, the founding chairman of the

Augusta National Golf Club, who hired two head professionals for the club in the sixties and told them that they'd better get along, because if he ever had to fire either of them, he was going to fire them both. The two worked together for almost forty years.)

When I opened the Bank of Dad, I told my kids that I would be delighted to provide them with printed account statements on demand, and for a long time I made a conscientious effort to categorize their expenditures and deposits in ways that I thought might intrigue them—a neat trick that Quicken and other banking programs make easy. (I am semi-compulsive about categorizing my own expenditures; I even have a category called "uncategorized," which I use for items that don't fit anywhere else.) Wouldn't the kids like to know, for example, exactly how much money they had spent on books, music, candy, and video games in the most recent quarter—or to study a bar graph illustrating how much loot they had taken in during each of the past four Christmases? But they turned out to have no curiosity whatsoever about those matters, and they never asked for printed statements or colorful, informative charts. The strictly clerical side of the Bank of Dad appealed enormously to me, but almost not at all to them. The kids were interested only in their current balances, their most recent interest payments, and whether I had remembered to adjust their allowances in accordance with some hard-fought recent negotiation. If I wasn't around, they would pull up their accounts on my computer and check for themselves.

At first, I felt disappointed that my kids showed so little interest in bookkeeping busywork. But I realized later that my disappointment was unjustified. The purpose of saving is for the depositors to be rewarded, not to let Dad play at being a banker. The rate of return was all that mattered to my kids, and it was all that should have mattered; my temporary obsession with forging a realistic deposit slip was my problem, not theirs. Overall lesson: The simpler I kept our bank, the better it worked.

THE PARTS THAT DON'T MATTER

Early in the history of the Bank of Dad, my kids and I would get together in my office on the last evening of the month to calculate their interest payments—an exercise that gave me an opportunity to show them a little about averages, percentages, and pocket calculators. But these sessions soon began to bore all of us, and after a few months my kids generally left me on my own to calculate their earnings. I eventually decided that that was O.K., too. After all, I expect the companies that look after my investments to take care of the bulk of my accounting. I don't have to go down to the bank every month and help a teller tot up my account. And I'm glad I don't.

If you start a bank for your own kids, I think you should remember the same thing. Once our children become adults, they will have plenty of time and motivation to learn about reconciling monthly bank statements, keeping tax records, and saving for no-fun future expenses like nursing-home room and board. Now is the time to get them interested in the exciting parts. If we do a good job of that, the responsibilities will take care of themselves. We don't want to scare our kids away from saving by making it seem like more trouble than it's worth. As my daughter said one day when she was not quite three, "'Responsibility' means 'very boring.'"

ACCOMMODATING THE NEEDS OF CHILDREN

Does it harm children to offer them a rate of return that in the adult world would be viewed as unrealistically high?

No.

Children have different needs and expectations, which we adults harmlessly accommodate in lots of ways—for example, by giving kids smaller chairs, more comfortable clothes, sweeter food, easier books, shorter skis, better-tasting toothpaste, and bicycles with training wheels. Such concessions to youth don't spoil our kids; they help our kids develop the skills and habits and confidence they will need later to lead successful lives as adults. We don't say to crawling babies, "Hey, just a minute there! You don't see me on my knees, do you?" Only when it comes to money do parents seem to expect their children from very early ages to be as sober and virtuous as adults (or, in fact, more sober and virtuous than adults). That's just wrong.

Nevertheless, I soon discovered that I had overreached with the initial interest rate of the Bank of Dad. After my bank had been in operation for less than two years, each of my children had managed to save more than four hundred dollars. Worried that their balances might soon soar out of control—especially now that my daughter was beginning to baby-sit—I called my children into my office and announced that I was reducing my monthly interest rate to 3 percent. They squawked at first, but they nodded solemnly as I explained the law of supply and demand and said that it applies even to the supply of money, pointing out that it would be bad for everyone if Dad's supply of money became exhausted. Changing the agreed-upon interest rate also gave me a chance to describe that fine old marketing strategy, bait-and-switch. (I still think 5 percent was a good teaser rate, though. I'd offer it again for the first year or two.)

The most amazing thing to me about the Bank of Dad is that it lasted for six years—far longer than the expected life span of almost any sort of ongoing family project. My kids never decided that my bank was stupid, and neither did I. They did finally outgrow it, when they became teenagers—and at that point we replaced it with a more grown-up alternative, as I'll explain in a later chapter. But by then they had both become committed savers. In fact, each had managed to pile up slightly more than a thousand dollars, despite having lived quite regally (as far as they were concerned) for the previous half-dozen years. When the time came to close my bank's doors, I did so without regret. My kids had learned from it everything that I had hoped they would learn.

BANKING AND SEX EDUCATION

My kids got the idea behind the Bank of Dad right away, even though when we began, neither one of them understood exactly what interest rates or percentages or even banks really were. That was fine with me. In fact, I don't think the underlying concepts need to be overexplained, especially to children who are very young. As Dr. Spock correctly observed about sex education, you shouldn't give kids more information than they really

need or want to know. A three-year-old who asks where babies come from isn't asking to be told about the part played by popular music and aftershave lotion.

I don't mean that kids aren't capable of understanding a lot. I just mean that well-meaning adults should resist any temptation to destroy their children's budding interest in fiscal responsibility by subjecting them to lectures on the workings of the Federal Reserve. My son, at the age of six, developed a vivid, intuitive understanding of interest rates simply by observing what happened month by month to his account in my bank—despite the fact that at school he and the rest of his class were still wrestling with addition and subtraction. He couldn't have told you what a percentage was, but he knew that if he built his balance to a hundred dollars, he would receive an extra five dollars at the end of the month. He also knew that if he left that new sum on deposit for one additional month, the same interest rate would apply not just to the original hundred bucks but to his entire cumulative balance—which by that point would include his allowance as well as the previous month's interest. In other words, he understood the miracle of compounding, even though he couldn't have come close to giving you a dictionary definition. (He can today, but not because of anything I taught him.)

Still, there may be times when you feel compelled to do some general explaining, especially if your kids ask

you for information. As always in such situations, it pays
to be prepared. (Quick! How does television work!) To
spare you embarrassment, I've done some of the preparation for you.

JUST WHAT IS A BANK, ANYWAY?

Young children deduce, early in their lives, that banks are
big, boring stores where grown-ups go to get money.
What the grown-ups have to do, if anything, in exchange
for that money is a mystery at first. I remember being
very little and overhearing my parents fretting about
how they were going to meet some horrible expense.
Jeez, I thought to myself, why don't you just go down to
that big marble building and grab some more dough?
(I'm paraphrasing.)

The time will undoubtedly come when your children
will want to know how banking really works. One way
to answer them, I think, is to pursue the idea of a bank as
a money store. That means you first have to tell them a
little bit about how stores work.

How *do* stores work? Well, stores sell stuff for money.
Where do they get the stuff they sell? They buy it, for
money, from companies that make stuff. (There's no need
to talk about distributors or middlemen or jobbers at this

point, in my opinion.) In order to stay in business, a store has to be able to sell stuff for more money than it pays for the stuff in the first place. Kids should have no trouble with that concept, especially if they themselves have ever been in the position of buying and selling Pokemon cards, Beanie Babies, comic books, video games, or anything else.

You can probably astonish your kids by telling them how relatively little a store usually pays for the stuff it sells, in comparison with the prices it charges. A doll that sells for twenty dollars in a toy store probably cost the toy store about ten dollars, assuming the standard retail markup of approximately 100 percent. Why such a big difference? Well (you can explain to your kids) just think of how much money the owners of a toy store have to spend just to stay in business. They have to pay money to rent the store itself, and they have to pay for power and heat and telephone lines, and they have to give salaries to their employees, and they have to buy advertising so customers will know what they have to sell, and so forth. The money for all those expenses has to come from the difference between what the store pays for toys (the wholesale price) and what it charges for toys (the retail price). If there's any money left over, the store has a profit; if the money runs out, the store has a loss.

Blockbuster Is a Kind of Bank

Another useful example—and one with which your kids are probably familiar—is Blockbuster. Blockbuster buys DVDs from companies that make DVDs, then rents those same DVDs to people like you and me. To stay in business, Blockbuster has to take in more money in rental fees (and candy sales) than it spends for DVDs (and candy), not to mention all those other expenses, like rent and electricity and salaries. This arrangement has advantages for everybody: you and I get to watch DVDs without having to pay full price for them (and without having to check a dozen different stores to find the ones we want); the people who work at Blockbuster get jobs, enabling them to earn the money they need to rent DVDs of their own; the companies that make DVDs get to sell lots of DVDs, and many more of them than they would if individual customers had to buy, rather than rent, any movie they wanted to watch; and the people who own Blockbuster get to make money—assuming, of course, that everything works the way it's supposed to.

Banks work very much the same way Blockbuster does. Instead of renting DVDs, though, banks are in the business of renting money. They do that by borrowing money from some people and then lending the same money to other people. When people deposit money in a bank, what they are really doing is lending money to the bank. In exchange, the bank protects their savings and pays them interest or lets them do things like write checks. Then the bank takes their money and lends it to people who need to borrow money, or invests it in other ways. The bank stays in business as long as it is able to charge more money to its borrowers than it has to pay to its lenders. Ta-dah! It's just like Blockbuster, but, instead of DVDs, think piles of money.

The real banking world is more complicated than that, of course, but the examples I've just given cover most of the essentials. If your children, for some reason, demand to know more, you can broaden their understanding of banking by telling them a little bit about how home mortgages work. (Here are the basic points: Houses cost so much that almost no one could afford to buy one if they had to pay for it in a single chunk; if everyone had to save the entire purchase price before buying a house, few people would still need shelter of any sort by the time they had finally scraped together enough money; banks solve this problem by lending home buyers very large amounts of money and then permitting them to pay back the money over very long periods of time. Banks earn fees and interest along the way, while borrowers get protection from the weather and—usually—a manageable payment schedule. When the system functions smoothly, everyone comes out ahead.)

What do *you* get out of operating a bank for your children? Like any banker, you get the use of your depositors' money for as long as it's on deposit. You do have to pay an onerous interest rate, but in return for your sacrifice, you receive the satisfaction of knowing that your kids are effortlessly equipping themselves to become fiscally responsible adults. And if you think about how much more expensive your own life would be if your children were fiscally irresponsible, the rate won't seem onerous at all.

3

RESPONSIBILITY AND CONTROL

DESPITE THE PREVIOUS CHAPTER'S EMPHASIS on high returns, the most significant feature of the Bank of Dad had nothing to do with interest rates. It had to do with control. My children's accounts belonged to them alone. When they saved, they reaped the benefit; when they wanted to spend, they didn't need permission. If my son decided to withdraw twenty dollars, I didn't ask him why he needed the money—just as my bank doesn't ask me. What he did with the cash was his business, as long as his balance was sufficient to cover his withdrawal.

Why do kids need to control money of their own? Because if the money they spend isn't truly theirs, they have no compelling reason to pay attention to how they spend it. My children are often quite irresponsible with my money, and why shouldn't they be? But they are extremely careful with their own.

I don't mean that anything goes at our house. My children aren't allowed to own narcotics or handguns, for example, and they can't substitute candy for vegetables at dinner, or watch TV in their rooms. But those are house behavior rules, not spending rules. Within the limits of permissible behavior, though, the kids are on their own. If my son wants to use his own money to buy some crummy item that I know is bound to fall apart, that decision is his, not mine. I might offer a little friendly advice based on my own extensive experience of making ill-conceived purchases—as I might to any friend—but I have no official veto power. If my kids want to spend their money foolishly, that's up to them.

This is a hard concept for most parents to accept. Can a nine-year-old (let's say) really be permitted to spend a hundred dollars or more on an MP3 player (for example)—a fragile piece of electronic equipment, which she will be fairly likely to break or lose within a month or two? My answer would be yes, if she's not acting under duress and if the money truly belongs to her. (Let's say it was a holiday present from a rich aunt.) I personally might not want to spend so much of my own money on an MP3 player for a nine-year-old— but that's my decision, because my money belongs to me. If the little girl in question wants to spend her own money in that way, though, then more power to her. She'll either take good care of her big purchase or she'll learn a lesson she won't soon forget.*

The mistake most parents make, I think, is to blur the boundary between their own money and that of their children, to the point where the children can only be irresponsible and annoying. If your own income consisted solely of what you were able to beg from a fickle and inscrutable boss, then you would wheedle, too. Children who have no control over their own funds have no incentive not to plead for money and then to squander every dollar that comes into their hands.

WHOSE MONEY IS IT?

When my kids were younger, I used to slip them a little extra pocket money when we went on vacation, maybe twenty or thirty bucks, to spend on trip-related items. But to make sure they thought of this extra money as theirs,

---

*There are obviously cases—and in some families this might be one of them—where the potential for regret and disappointment is so huge that parents can't bear to butt out, and therefore shouldn't. But the general principle still holds, and the mere fact that a desired purchase may be foolhardy does not automatically justify parental intervention.

not mine, I gave it to them before we left home (by depositing it in their accounts in the Bank of Dad), and told them that they could spend it on a souvenir T-shirt when we were on vacation, save it forever, spend it on baseball cards before we left, lose it, or do anything else they wanted with it—but that while we were on vacation they would receive no additional funds from me (except in the form of communal purchases considered by family custom to be vacation entitlements, such as ice cream, movie tickets, miniature-golf green fees, and so on).

Because any money they spent during the trip therefore belonged to them, they thought twice before throwing it away. In a souvenir store on Martha's Vineyard one summer, my son, who was seven at the time, quietly studied the unpromising merchandise while a friend of his loudly cajoled his parents into paying five dollars for a toy tomahawk. My son ended up spending thirty-three cents for an unopened geode, which he later opened by whacking it with a hammer—a good value, even from my jaded perspective. If he had been spending my money instead of his, he undoubtedly would have wanted a toy tomahawk instead. (The geodes were actually being sold three for a dollar; my son didn't want to spend that much, so he talked the proprietor into breaking a set and selling him just one—a negotiation in which I was not involved.)

I didn't have to give my son a lecture on the shoddiness of toy tomahawks. He could see their flaws as easily as I could, because for him there was no emotional dimension to the transaction. The other child was less interested in possessing a tomahawk than in winning a loud, public battle of wills with his parents, and he knew from past experience that if he made a big enough stink, they would eventually give in. His fascination with the tomahawk ended the instant his father pulled out his wallet. Indeed, the tomahawk was broken before we got back to the car.

Advanced Parenting

One often sees (and, perhaps, participates in) similar psychodramas—for example, at the supermarket. A bored young child, wearing a snow jacket, a knit cap, and mittens, trudges along in perspiry silence until the family shopping cart is nearly full, then begins to beg for candy, gum, a comic book, or something similar. The beleaguered supervising parent, who doesn't want to seem weak-willed in the eyes of total strangers, feigns deafness; the child cranks up the volume; the parent vaguely threatens future punishment; the child begins to cry and perhaps also to stamp the floor or hang morosely from the front of the cart. The scene ends either in physical violence or in total parental capitulation, while childless adults in adjacent checkout lines smugly pretend to read the cover of the *National Enquirer.*

Avoiding such scenes is usually possible. The first step is to acknowledge that taking a young child on a boring shopping expedition has many benefits for a parent, who is able to get the shopping done without arranging for childcare or surrendering personal time, but no benefits for the child, who would prefer to be doing almost anything else. If the roles were reversed, the parent would almost certainly feel entitled to compensation. ("We've played a good long game of Timothy the Horse, and now Daddy needs to lie on the couch and watch the baseball game for half an hour.") Doesn't it seem fair to offer compensation to the child?

I think it does. The trick with young children, though, is to make sure that the compensation is tangible, immediate, and truly under their control. One way to do that is to hire the child, in effect, as a shopping companion. You might say something like this: "I need to do a big, boring grocery shopping, and I need for you to come with me. Before we go to the store, I am going to give you two dollars, which you may spend on a treat for yourself at the store, or save, or do whatever you like with. But I need for you to behave yourself in the store, and if you don't, I'm going to take the money back." Paying in advance is important, I think, because it eliminates the child's suspicion (often justified) that after a hellishly boring hour, you will fabricate some reason not to pay up. Also, money in one's pocket seems infinitely more real than money in someone else's, and is therefore a more powerful incentive.

Naturally, the size and nature of the bribe must be adjusted to the age and canniness of the child. When our kids were very little, we would sometimes keep them tractable on trips to the supermarket by telling them that if they behaved, they could each choose "one small book" (at a price of a couple of dollars) from the supermarket's depressing book section. Selecting their books often kept them occupied until almost all the groceries had been rounded up, and reading the books or flipping through the pages kept both children quiet on the drive home—an excellent value for all.

HOW TO NEGOTIATE WITH CHILDREN

Giving a child an incentive in advance is very different from promising the child that you will buy him or her a "treat" if the child is "good." This sort of attempted bribe often leads to another fraught negotiation, as the parent feels compelled to veto one suggested payoff after another ("too expensive"; "too sweet"; "too close to dinner"), and the child begins to feel had.* If there are nonobvious ground rules in transactions between parents and children, the ground rules should be explained in advance.

A good example of this type of payment-in-advance was described to me by another parent. This woman and her husband had recently thrown a big dinner party, and they hadn't been able to find a baby-sitter for their two young sons. The mom told the boys that she wanted them to play upstairs until it was time for them to be tucked into bed, and not to make a nuisance of themselves or wander irritably among the guests. She gave each of the boys five one-dollar bills, and told them that the money was their reward, paid in advance, for being, in effect, their own baby-sitters. However, she said, she would take back one dollar from each of them every time they came downstairs in a nonemergency or made a ruckus that required parental intervention.

As you might expect, both boys behaved like angels. They knew the money was really theirs, because they could see it in their hands, and they didn't want to lose it. They played quietly upstairs, reveling in their riches, until it was time to go to bed.

There is obviously some danger that a crafty child will attempt to monetize traditionally gratis family functions,

---

*I myself would happily look the other way while a young child of mine ate sugar out of a bag if doing so would buy me thirty uninterrupted minutes; other parents may disagree.

by demanding payment for showing up at the dinner
table, say, or for going to bed on time. But you can control that danger by behaving the way parents are supposed to behave—that is, by being firm. You can explain
to your kids that having tedious responsibilities is just a
normal part of life, for children as well as for adults, and
that no one gets paid for shouldering all of them. In
other words: no payments for remembering to flush the
toilet (although you might, as you neared the end of your
wits, impose a fine for not remembering). Still, there are
instances in which rewards are justified, and regular grocery-store expeditions and big boring grown-up parties
seem to me like two of them.

THE BENEFITS OF SHARING POWER

Having real control of their own money forces children
to confront and weigh their actual desires. It also frees
parents from having to play an invariably judgmental and
adversarial role in the family economy. If my daughter
thinks she might like to add some expensive accessory to
her room, she doesn't have to persuade me that the purchase would be a good idea; she has to persuade herself.
And if she decides to ask my advice, she knows that my
opinion won't be tainted by my well-known reluctance

to spend money on purchases that don't do me any good (although that opinion will no doubt still reflect my broad ignorance of the desires of teenage girls). Because we have established a reasonably clear division between my resources and hers, the process can play itself out rationally. The question my daughter has to answer is not "How can I talk Dad into paying for this?" but "Is this something I really want?"

Allowing children to accumulate and control money of their own permits parents to recuse themselves from much unpleasant decision-making. "I won't buy that for you, but you have enough money to buy it for yourself if you really want it" is a pronouncement I have pronounced so often around my house that both my children now mock me cruelly. But they know they're better off than they were before they achieved a semblance of financial independence, and their freedom frees me, too. Is a particular piece of jewelry or a video game "worth it"? What parent can say? But my wife and I are no longer the ones who have to decide.

When my kids were young, they decided between themselves that they would like to own a CD-burner—a pricey novelty at the time. They told me that if I would spring for the device and install it on any one of our family's growing herd of computers, they would make CDs for me whenever I wanted them, enabling me to rapidly earn back my investment—about three hundred dollars—in the form of homemade disks containing my favorite songs. I told the kids that I was interested in having access to a CD-burner but not in paying for the whole thing myself, since the principal beneficiaries of the deal would undoubtedly be the two of them. They saw my point. After a brief negotiation, we agreed to split the cost three ways. We also agreed that I would handle the installation, on one of their computers, and that they would make CDs for me whenever I asked.

This negotiation went exactly the way family financial negotiations ought to go, I think. I knew what a CD-burner was worth to me, and my kids knew what it was worth to them—and we arrived at our opinions without anyone's having to whine, wheedle, or scream. Such an outcome would have been impossible if the children hadn't had absolute control over money of their own. I knew they were serious, because they were willing to spend large sums of real money that they themselves had saved. (I was especially proud of them for figuring out a way to persuade me to pick up part of the tab.) We all behaved rationally, and we all came out ahead.

Needs and Desires

My son and I once had a similar negotiation regarding his bicycle. After seeing a brand-new bike belonging to a friend of his, he decided that he was no longer satisfied with his own, and he told me that he needed a new one. I told him that I thought his current bike (which had been a gift from me and his mother) was terrific, and that he hadn't outgrown it yet, and that I didn't think he needed an upgrade. However, I said, "Your current bike is still valuable, and you have saved some money as well. If you trade in your bike, or sell it and apply the proceeds to the purchase price, you can afford to buy a new one. Your decision—not mine." He soberly considered all the angles and decided he didn't need a new bike after all. Because he was in control, he was free to behave rationally.

If my son had not been in control of assets of his own, our discussion, no matter how it ended up, would have had to be based on emotion alone:

"I need a new bike!"

"No, you don't!"

"Yes, I do!"

"No, you don't!"

"Yes, I do!"

"No, you don't!"

"Yes, I do!"

"No, you don't!"

All such arguments inevitably bog down on irrelevant and ultimately irresolvable issues, such as whether twenty-seven gears is really enough, or whether aluminum is even remotely comparable to titanium, or whether a friend's bike really is or isn't better. (Shifting the focus of an argument away from the main issue is a good rhetorical tactic, by the way, if you ever find yourself forced to defend an indefensible position in a fight with your children.)

But the point is not to settle the question of whether a new bike would be "better"—obviously, it would be. The point is to decide whether "better" is worth the price. That decision can be made only by the person who controls the dough, and it can be made fairly only if the person who controls the dough is also the person who stands to benefit from the expenditure.

This principle is extremely important, because responsibility is impossible without control. Children who feel a strong sense of ownership are far more likely to take care of their possessions than children who don't. A bicycle is more than just a form of transportation, if it is perceived by the child who rides it as a store of value, or, at upgrade time, as a form of currency. Even if my son loses interest in riding his bike, he will still understand that the bike is his, and that it contributes to his economic well-being, and that if he leaves it out in the rain, it will be worth less and he will therefore be poorer. A sense of ownership is what makes grown-ups treat their own cars better than they treat rental cars. We want to encourage our kids to act like the owners of their own possessions rather than mere renters. We certainly don't want to encourage them to act like squatters.

The Limits of Freedom

Control isn't always a simple issue. There are many instances in which a parent may feel a strong need to retain authority over expenditures that might otherwise be treated as discretionary, and in such instances the parent should be prepared to pay up. For example, if your seventeen-year-old son earns enough money over a couple of summers to buy a car of his own, you might commend him for his diligence but invoke a sort of parental version of the doctrine of eminent domain, and declare yourself the owner of the car's seat belts, air bags, brakes, and tires. You might also appoint yourself to serve as the chief justice of your family's own traffic court, with the express power to suspend the driving privileges of careless teens—even those who own their own car.

Financial independence in young people is a good

thing, but major safety issues shouldn't be decided on the basis of the contents of a teenager's wallet. If the tires are bald, you want to be sure they get replaced—and promptly. The best way to do that is to own them yourself. You can let your son retain title to most of the rest of the car. But you can also make it clear that for as long as his welfare is largely your responsibility, there will be no skimping on brake fluid, and that violations of commonly accepted safe-driving standards will be severely punished.

Exactly how you might work out the financial details of such an agreement depends on a huge number of factors, including your own resources, the general responsibility level of your children, and the way in which your family typically divvies up financial obligations. I'll have more to say on this subject in the next chapter, which concerns allowances.

4

ALLOWANCES

EVERY CHILD WHO IS OLD ENOUGH to be vaguely aware of the existence and function of money (and yet is no longer so young as to be interested in swallowing pennies) should receive an allowance. Children need money of their own, and paying them an allowance is the best and easiest way to ensure that they have it. I don't recall how old my children were when I gave them their first allowances, but I hope they were very young.

Different people have different ideas about children's allowances, but certain notions are held almost universally by thoughtful parents. Among the more significant of these widely held notions: a child's allowance should be set low enough to prevent the child from spending foolishly; a child should be required to save some portion of every allowance payment; a child should be required to give to charity some portion of every allowance payment; a child's allowance should be linked to the satisfactory completion of certain household obligations, such as emptying the trash.

I disagree with all of these ideas. I'll discuss them one at a time.

HOW BIG SHOULD A CHILD'S ALLOWANCE BE?

Among parents there is a strong and largely unconscious desire to keep children in a condition of enforced semipoverty. Money is at least partly a control issue in most families, and children who don't have much money seem easier to control, since they have limited opportunities for autonomous action. There is also a widespread feeling among adults, perhaps traceable to our grimly destitute Pilgrim forefathers, that deprivation is good for the soul.

My own feeling is that keeping children on excessively short financial leashes promotes fiscal irresponsibility. There is a very funny series of British children's books (written between the 1920s and the 1970s by a woman named Richmal Crompton) about an eleven-year-old boy named William Brown, who, among other perennial difficulties, never has enough money. His official allowance is infinitesimal, and he seldom receives even that, because his father is continually docking him for the cost of property he has damaged or of possessions he has ruined or lost. As a consequence, on the rare occasions when he and his friends do suddenly acquire a few pennies, they unburden themselves immediately and impetuously, before some malicious adult can think of an excuse to empty their pockets for them. They are not savers. Their financial planning extends no further than the end of the day. When they grow up, they will max out their credit cards.

Children who receive harshly stingy allowances, as William Brown does, have no reason to think long-term. They see no point in saving, or in comparing possible purchases, because they know that their incomes are too meager ever to accumulate into anything significant. When such children do come into money, they tend to spend it heedlessly; the rest of the time, they rely on whining, cajoling, and birthday presents to carry them through. They know nothing about money except that money never seems to have anything to do with them.

In order to be transformed into responsible spenders, such children need to be given opportunities to spend. They need to have chances to make wise and foolish decisions, and they need to be given those chances fairly often, so that the difference between wisdom and foolishness will come to strike them as both real and important. To children who control little or no money of their own, the sudden appearance or disappearance of a ten-dollar bill is just an act of God: it's unfathomable and unpredictable, so why make plans? I didn't begin to become truly responsible with my own money until I had enough of it to squander some every once in a while.

There's a certain grave discipline in just scraping by, of course, but poverty is a sharply limited teacher. What you want your kids to learn is not how to muddle along with nothing but how to intelligently manage a simulacrum of the affluence you hope they will someday achieve as working adults. You want to help them prepare themselves mentally for the moment in their adult lives when they will have ceased to be struggling graduate students and have begun to earn more money than the bare minimum they need to cover the groceries and the rent. You want to help them get better at making intelligent choices, and the only way you can do that is to give them opportunities to choose—and, not incidentally, chances to screw up.

How much allowance should a child receive? The precise amount depends on many nonformulaic factors, including the prosperity of the parents, the age and maturity of the child, the child's other sources of income, if any, the kinds of financial responsibilities the child is expected to assume, and—especially—the size of allowances received by classmates and friends. But here's a general guideline that makes sense to me: a child's personal financial resources (which include periodic cash gifts from relatives, baby-sitting money, and other forms of income) ought to add up, annually, to a sum that the child perceives to be more than enough. An allowance, that is, should be large enough to permit spending beyond whatever is absolutely necessary (and saving, too, if attractive opportunities are available), although it shouldn't be so large as to seem either unreal or inexhaustible. My son's very mature and rational decision not to trade up to a new bicycle (a decision I described in the previous chapter) would have been meaningless if he had not been given an opportunity, over what to him seemed like a reasonable period of time, to save enough money to make the transaction feasible. His decision also would have been meaningless if he had somehow piled up so much money that the choice could have meant nothing at all to him. (One of my children once had a friend who carelessly dropped wads of cash around his room, like old, smelly socks; that's way too much money.)

Ideally, I think, children should probably feel neither rich nor poor in relation to the majority of their peers, but vaguely "comfortable" (assuming their parents are in a position to let them feel that way). If they lose the equivalent of a week's allowance, they should feel remorseful and upset; if they find the equivalent of a week's allowance, their first impulse should not be to run out and blow it all immediately on candy.

The best way to begin to set allowances is often to ask the children themselves what they think they ought to receive, and which of their expenses they think they ought to personally assume. Both of mine, years ago, surprised me by asking for less than I would have offered. (Most children, like most adults, underestimate their expenses.) We arrived at their current allowances through trial and error and a succession of friendly negotiations, and both children understand that the amounts they receive could be adjusted up or down at any time, should conditions change. (At my request, when my children seek allowance increases, they do so in writing, enumerating the reasons—a terrifically useful exercise. Additional benefit: it is almost impossible to whine on paper.) They both currently spend less than they take in. That's proof, in my view, that their allowances are probably about right.

The younger your children are when you begin paying them an allowance, the more easily you'll be able to settle on appropriate amounts as they grow older, because as the years go by you'll acquire more and more information about their needs, their habits, and their weaknesses. You'll also have more opportunities to swap ideas with the parents of their friends. And your kids will have a much clearer idea of what seems fair to them.

Obviously, there are dozens, if not hundreds or thousands, of exceptions to all of this. Kids who have or may have drug problems probably can't be given regular access to more than a dribble of cash; kids who hate to spend anything may need to be coaxed into loosening up; kids who believe in spending first and asking questions later may need to be brought around gradually. The overall goal should be to give them some room to maneuver, so they can discover true responsibility all by themselves. How much freedom they can reasonably handle can be determined only by you and them. (My general advice: err on the side of more freedom rather than less.)

SHOULD CHILDREN BE REQUIRED TO SAVE SOME PART OF THEIR ALLOWANCES?

No. Saving is meaningless unless it's voluntary. That's what Chapters 2 and 3 are about. If you automatically impound a chunk of your kids' allowances every month and whisk it off to the bank, your kids will never think of the confiscated chunk as theirs—especially if your intention is to spend "their" savings on college or some other expense in the (to them) distant future. If you offer your children true control of their money and a sufficiently attractive rate of return, they'll save all by themselves.

Giving older children attractive, meaningful opportunities for saving can be tricky. In Chapter 6, I'll describe some ways in which I think it can be done.

SHOULD OLDER CHILDREN BE REQUIRED TO GIVE AWAY SOME PART OF THEIR ALLOWANCES?

Again, no. Charity isn't charity if the gift is not the giver's to give. When parents require their children to give away a certain amount of money every week or every month, the parents are really just craftily confiscating what they believe to be excess resources. It's the parents who are making the gift, not the kids. If you pay your child a weekly allowance of ten dollars but require him to put one dollar in the church plate and two dollars in an untouchable passbook account, then his weekly allowance is really seven dollars, and he knows it.

Charity and coercion are mutually exclusive. The way to teach charity is not by fiat but by example. If your children see you cheerfully giving away some of your own money or possessions or labor or time, they will get the idea all by themselves. And the younger your children are when you begin to set these admirable examples, the quicker and more eagerly they will catch on.

Without bragging about yourself too much, you

should give your children opportunities to see you being generous with your own resources. Explain to them—occasionally and, if possible, modestly—why you contribute to the Red Cross or give old clothes to Goodwill or serve on the board of a local charity. And tell them not only what you hope your contributions do for others but also what you think they do for you. Don't get preachy; just let your kids see that caring about others is a regular, natural part of your life. If you don't screw up too badly, caring about others will probably become a regular, natural part of their lives, too.

Young children, especially, don't need much nudging when it comes to giving of themselves. When I first asked my daughter, at the age of four and a half, if she would like to have a savings account at a regular bank, she asked, "Will poor people be able to get my money?"

"No," I said, "the money in your account will belong only to you."

"I would like for poor people to get some of it," she said.

"That's very nice of you," I said. "Mommy and I give away some of our money. It's a good thing to do."

"I would like to do that, too," she said. "They could use it to buy some keys, or a car."

She's old enough now to have her own checkbook and credit card (not to mention her own keys and a car), and she still gives away money without any prompting from me or her mother or anyone else. Judging by the kind of junk mail she receives, I would guess that her favorite causes are not necessarily my favorite causes. But that's her business.

Both of my children think of making charitable gifts and performing charitable acts as personal obligations. But they arrived at those beliefs without parental coercion. Our job as parents is to help our children prepare themselves for the day—which inevitably arrives sooner than anyone ever thinks—when we can't boss them around anymore. If we make giving seem like a punishment, they will rebel as soon as they are on their own. But if we make giving seem natural and admirable and even personally rewarding, they will pick it up all by themselves.

SHOULD CHILDREN HAVE TO EARN THEIR ALLOWANCES BY PERFORMING CERTAIN CHORES?

This is a touchy one with many parents—but usually for the wrong reasons. I believe that children should be given allowances, and I believe that children should do household chores, but I don't believe the two activities should be linked.

Doing most chores around the house is not a job; it's

just a regular family obligation, and every able-bodied member should have to pitch in to some extent, no questions asked. (For exceptions, see page 68.) If you believe that it's important for your children to make their beds every morning, for example, then you should not suggest to them or to yourself that you need to pay them to make them do it.* The standard mundane activities that keep any household running smoothly should be shared, at age-appropriate levels of involvement, by all capable helpers, and that's that.

Linking a chore to an allowance turns the chore into a job, and that creates the possibility that the worker might someday decide to retire. Most kids never make that conceptual leap, but they easily could. "I'm feeling pretty flush right now," your son might suddenly say, "so I've decided to stop cleaning up after myself for the time being. Why don't you spend my next few allowances on something nice for yourself?" In truth, an allowance that is linked to the completion of household chores isn't

---

*Bed-making has never quite caught on in our household, except with our daughter, who never fails to make hers and never needs to be reminded—not that any other member of our family would have the moral authority to comment on the bed-maintenance habits of anyone else. For unknown reasons, my wife and I seem slightly more likely to make our bed just before getting into it than we are to make it immediately after getting out of it. I also have a theory that bed-making skips generations, since both my wife and I were required to make our beds when we were kids.

really anything like a wage; it's just a mild form of ransom—and the practice can backfire.

I also think that it is usually a mistake for parents to establish or even suggest a link between school performance and allowance or any other form of monetary compensation—something parents often do. Paying for grades almost always causes more problems than it solves. The practice insidiously shifts the responsibility for doing well in school from the (working) student to the (paying) parent, and it opens sweeping new battlegrounds for psychological warfare. The last thing in the world you should do is to create the possibility that your child might decide one morning that she is going to stop listening carefully in English this semester because she no longer needs the cash. Nor do you want your son to develop a take-this-job-and-shove-it attitude about passing algebra.

I do believe that it's O.K. to pay children for performing household jobs that fall outside the category of ordinary chores, though. Some jobs are too crummy, too big, too irregular, or too specialized to be treated as merely obligatory—annually cleaning out the dog run, for example, or rescuing a grown-up's hopelessly muddled hard drive, or mowing the lawn (a job that would cost you plenty if you had to hire it out on the open market). Besides, most kids need and, occasionally, welcome opportunities to earn money beyond whatever they have managed to husband from their allowances and other income sources. Fair warning: the parent-child employment relationship is fraught with emotional booby traps, and young children tend to be appalled when they discover the real length of an hour.

For similar reasons, I think that children should be paid—and at the local market rate—when they baby-sit for siblings. Doing so establishes the idea that being left in charge is a privilege, not a punishment. (Besides, you pay potentially unreliable strangers to baby-sit; why not your own perfect kids?) Furthermore, I think that such baby-sitting payments should be divided in some equitable fashion between sitters and sittees, if the latter are old enough to behave better when offered cash incentives but not yet old enough to be left on their own. Paying both parties greatly reduces intra-family resentment—an especially big problem when sitters are only slightly older than their closely related charges. (Once all the children at home are mature enough to be left alone, they don't need to be paid anymore for keeping an eye on one another, or on themselves. In fact, at that point most of them would probably be happy to pay you to leave the house.)

Maintaining separation between regular chores and optional piecework is admittedly tricky. When my wife was a teen, her father paid her to mow the lawn every week, a time-consuming responsibility that she hated, in part because her father was meticulous about his yard.

One day, she asked him if she could do a worse job and be paid less. That proposal annoyed her father deeply, as you can probably imagine, but her question was economically astute, and it revealed the flaw in the working arrangement her father had devised: mowing the lawn in my wife's family was not a true job, because the (sole) employee lacked the power to quit. In a genuinely free market, my wife's father would have had to meet her demand or find a more compliant worker to take her place. Instead, they had a fight.

HUMAN NATURE AGAIN

Parents have a self-defeating tendency to think of almost all the household chores they assign their children as a form of general punishment, which they impose for the purpose of reminding their unappreciative offspring how difficult and complicated life truly is. Keeping a household running is a damn lot of work, and if the kids aren't part of the solution, then they are definitely part of the problem—that's how most parents think, at least subconsciously. Putting kids to work around the house is a way of forcing the kids to acknowledge how much trouble their parents go to in creating such a wonderful life for everyone who sleeps under the roof.

It's often more productive, when assigning chores to children, to think first about harnessing the children's own self-interest, which can be an extraordinarily powerful force if you know where to find it. Grown-ups willingly do mind-numbing chores of all kinds (paying the bills, raking the leaves, scraping old paint off the shutters) because they can easily see the connection between their efforts and their own well-being. If I keep the exterior of my house in good condition, my thinking goes, then my long-term maintenance expenses will be lower, and the value of my property will increase, and my neighbors won't give me dirty looks when they pass me on the street. Those are powerful incentives for an adult, but they don't have much meaning for most children, especially young ones—nor should they. Expecting your eight-year-old to care about the condition of your storm windows with the same sense of urgency that you yourself feel is unrealistic and, therefore, counterproductive.

You will extract far more useful labor from your children, and help turn them into better people in the long run, if you pay attention to their needs and interests as well as to your own. Here are a few examples:

- Young kids don't necessarily view tidiness as an improvement. That's one reason why they let their rooms get out of hand. And once they finally do decide that messiness is a problem, the mess is usually so huge that attacking it seems hopeless. To find a way out of this bind, they will probably need assistance from you.

The most effective way to help them see the benefits of orderliness—and thereby help them to become entirely self-sufficient in this department—is to treat room-cleaning not as a punishment for slovenliness ("You go to your room and stay there until it doesn't look like a pigpen anymore!") but as the key to a better life. Doing that will require you yourself to pitch in initially, and to focus your first efforts on the parts of the job that are the most likely to produce obvious benefits for them.

One day when my daughter was very little, for example, we ignored the general, overwhelming mess in her playroom and tackled just the closet—a chore that was sufficiently circumscribed not to seem impossible to a three-year-old. As we worked our way through the disorder, which had been hidden for months behind a closed door, we came across many toys that she had forgotten about—and we stopped to play with most of them. We threw away lots of old junk, and we organized what was left, and we both had fun. To her, cleaning the closet that day seemed more like a treasure hunt than a reprimand: she could see the point. And the fact that she enjoyed the job didn't weaken her character; it helped to persuade her that cleaning up her stuff had benefits for her.

Our adventure in the closet also reinforced what may be the most important chore-related lesson of all, which is that incremental efforts pay off. Big jobs often look too big to even start—especially to young children, but also sometimes to grown-ups. You can help your kids (and perhaps yourself) by showing them that small efforts add up, and that big jobs can be tackled successfully if you first break them into manageable bits. Doing that is not mollycoddling. What you are really doing is making a steady, long-term investment in your children's life-management skills—itself an incremental chore.

- Before going on big family car trips, my kids and I would always give our minivan a thorough interior cleaning. I never presented this chore as a punishment, or pointed out that most of the mess we were cleaning up was a mess that had been created by them. We always simply treated cleaning up the car as something we did to get ready to go on vacation—and as a chore that made us all feel, happily, that our departure for the beach was at hand.

It would have made more sense, hygienically speaking, to conduct our annual major cleanup of the car immediately upon returning from vacation—when the car was full of sand and candy wrappers and two weeks' worth of accumulated trip detritus—but that chore would have seemed too depressing even for me. Doing it beforehand made the job seem both fun and immediately beneficial for all concerned, and it kept everyone interested in the result.

• Acquiring a driver's license elevated my daughter's level of personal interest in all car-related aspects of her life. Not long after she began driving, I pointed out to her that if the two of us spent an hour or two cleaning up the garage— which at that time was so full of trash cans and snow shovels and autumn leaves and indescribable junk that I could barely squeeze my own car inside it—she would be able to keep her car under the protection of a roof rather than in the driveway, where she was parking it at the time. She tackled the job with enthusiasm, and we made the garage a showplace. She later kept her half immaculate without pressure from me.

- While we were visiting my in-laws several years ago, my wife's father asked my son, who was seven or eight at the time, to sweep the leaves off the roof of his porch, a job that required my son to climb onto the roof through a bedroom window. He liked going out the window, and he liked being on the roof by himself, and he appreciated the fact that he had been given a serious, grown-up assignment. As a consequence, he worked hard and steadily, and he did a very good job.

Lesson: if you give your kids chores that flatter them by making them feel truly useful rather than merely exploited, they'll work harder, and—much more important—they'll understand why chores are good for all.

Please note: I'm not arguing that children should be assigned only chores that appeal to them; I'm just suggesting that if you are sensitive to your children's own self-interest when you put them to work around the house, they will work harder and require less supervision, and, with a little luck, they will begin to tackle useful jobs on their own initiative, without any nagging from you. If you make an effort not to treat chores as a form of punishment—a chore in itself for many parents—your children will respond favorably. You work around your house because you perceive the benefit to yourself; you can help your children develop a sense of enlightened self-interest, too—but doing so will require some thought and some creativity on your part, because your children's self-interest, in this case, will be harder to pinpoint than will your own.

KEEPING TRACK OF ALLOWANCE PAYMENTS

Did I receive my allowance last week, or not? I recall mulling that question repeatedly when I was a lad. I could often turn uncertainty to my advantage, since my parents were even less likely than I was to remember whether or not I had been paid.

A possible solution would have been to employ a system suggested by one well-known domestic-finance adviser: give each child a booklet containing fifty-two dated allowance vouchers, each redeemable for the agreed-upon weekly payment. That solution sounds kind of elegant, but I personally think it's too fussy to work for very long in most households. My kids have trouble keeping track of their shoes from one day to the next; what chance would they have of hanging on to a handful of slips of paper for an entire year? Besides, keeping track of payment dates ought to be the responsibility of the payer, not the payee. You would grumble if your employer handed you a stack of salary vouchers on January 1 and told you that you'd better not lose them.

The truly simple solution, I think, is to eliminate entirely the human-memory requirement from the allowance-payment system. If you use your computer to operate a bank for your kids, you can set it up so that their allowances are credited automatically at regular intervals. (If you operate your own bank but do the record-keeping manually, you can do the same thing on paper.) If your kids are old enough to have checking accounts at a real bank, you can set up automatic weekly or monthly transfers from your account to theirs. That's what I do now, and it's very straightforward. Automating allowances also keeps the process emotionally clean: your kids don't have to ask (or beg) for payments that you've already agreed to.

ALLOWANCES FOR OLDER CHILDREN

Allowance issues become more complicated as children themselves become more complicated. Teenagers have larger and less easily definable financial needs than preschoolers do, what with cars and popularity and sex and all. If your kids have been receiving regular allowances for years, by the time they become fierce adolescents, an equitable system may evolve all by itself. Or you may have to check around to find out what other parents are paying their kids these days, then ask your own kids what they think they need. Maybe they'll surprise you.

When my daughter was thirteen or fourteen, she decided that she wanted a clothing allowance, and we gave that idea a try for a while but found it impossible to work out to everyone's satisfaction. There were many complicating factors. The main one, not surprisingly, had to do with control. If you make your children responsible for paying for their own clothes, you are also inevitably making them responsible for deciding what they're going to wear. Items that generally seem essential to parents—untorn jeans, decent shoes, warm winter coats—may be viewed as optional by budget-conscious teens. My daughter's case was further complicated by the fact that her school had a strictly enforced but somewhat loosely defined dress code. These and other circumstances made it impossible for all of us to agree from one week to the next on a reasonable wardrobe or a reasonable budget or a reasonable division of responsibilities.

After a certain amount of fumbling around, we decided that my wife and I would pay for (and thus retain at least nominal control over) what we considered to be an adequate basic wardrobe for school and formal occasions, while leaving our daughter both the freedom and the resources to fill out the rest of her closet on her own. This system, if you can call it that, seemed to work fairly well, although its outlines were vague and its rules were inconsistently applied.

When my son got to be about the same age, he requested an allowance increase to cover, among other things, a modest level of discretionary clothes buying. In other words, he proposed essentially the same arrangement that my wife and I had eventually reached, through trial and error, with our daughter. For him, that system worked pretty well. My wife and I retained responsibility for making sure he didn't embarrass us by looking like a waif or a juvenile delinquent at school or in church, and he controlled what he looked like at those times when what he looked like mattered the most to him. A good, functional system—but impossible to turn into a formula. You'll have to feel your way around. (Now our son is in college, and we no longer have a vote.)

Overall, I believe that children are most likely to abide by the terms of family financial arrangements if they themselves have proposed those arrangements, or at least been allowed to take part in working out the details. Participating in the process also forces them to make a real effort to evaluate their financial needs and their spending habits—always a good thing. Requiring them to put their requests in writing ensures that you'll have a permanent record (and therefore a reminder) of each significant change.

What Should an Allowance Cover?

Who pays for what? Are clothes included? What about movies? Birthday presents? School supplies? Holiday gifts for people your children have never met? Ice cream on vacation?

Every family has to settle these complicated issues for itself. Here's a general suggestion, though: if you intend to retain control over certain purchase categories, the responsibility for paying for those purchases should also belong to you. Under ideal circumstances, children's spending should be entirely discretionary; that is, spending or not spending the money they control should be entirely up to them. If you decide to make them responsible for buying their own school supplies, then you have also decided to make them responsible for deciding whether or not they can bluff their way through the rest of geometry without a protractor.

In other words, the owner pays. If you are the one who decides what your children are allowed to wear, for example, then you should be the one to pay for their clothes. You own the decision, so you pay. Here are a few other examples:

- *Birthday presents for friends:* If there's a birthday party, the parent pays for the present. Why? Because you would never let your eight-year-old decide to economize on a friend's birthday present by slapping a bow on some old broken thing from under his bed. If your kid takes a crummy present to a birthday party, the other parents will criticize you, not him, so you have no choice but to retain control. And if you control, you pay.

The same goes when children of any age are invited to special events that traditionally involve big-ticket gift-giving: confirmations, bar mitzvahs, weddings, graduations. Parents should pay for those gifts, because the expenditures are too big and unpredictable to be budgeted in advance, and you yourself would be embarrassed if your child decided to cut back.

- *Presents for family members:* I don't think it's fair to make young children cover the cost of holiday, birthday, or other gifts for siblings, parents, grandparents, or other family members. Such expenditures tend to come in bunches and add up in a hurry, and they are therefore impossible for little kids to plan ahead for. The simplest solution by far is to pick up the tab—and supervise the shopping—yourself. (When our kids were little, our local library conducted an annual children's Christmas sale, at which kids shopped all by themselves, without help from their own parents, for inexpensive gifts for friends and family members—and wrapped them, too! One year when my daughter was very young, she asked me if I'd like to know what she had picked out for me. I said I'd rather be surprised, but she gave me a hint anyway. "-It's something that cuts," she said. Then she moved her fingers like a pair of scissors, and said, "Snip, snip, snip.")

Once children reach a certain age, however—somewhere in their teens, let's say—family gift-buying should become their responsibility, as long as their allowances are set at a sufficiently high level to cover such expenditures. (They will probably still need to be reminded of important dates well in advance, and maybe also given help with gift ideas.) At around that age, too, all gift-buying for their friends should become their financial responsibility alone—with the exception of the aforementioned big-ticket special events.

- *Family treats:* If you're present and a part of the outing, then you pay. That means that if you go along to the movie or the restaurant or the amusement park, you are the host. It would be much too disgusting to take your kids out for ice cream and then expect them to pull out their own wallets—especially if you yourself were happily pigging out on a banana split and they decided they couldn't afford to join you. Noblesse oblige.

On the other hand, you are perfectly within your rights to draw the line somewhere. When we went to Disney World, for example, I figured that airfare, food, lodging, Magic Kingdom tickets, and so forth were my wife's and my responsibility, but that crummy souvenirs were our children's. Added bonus: I never had to offer my opinion about the crumminess of the available souvenirs.

- *Family rules:* When my son was eleven, he decided that he wanted to own a kind of skateboard called an all-terrain board, which has big soft tires and is meant to be used on uneven ground, such as steep hills with rocks at the bottom. He had saved enough money to pay for it, but all-terrain boards are dangerous, so my wife and I retained veto power. We told him that we would permit him to own and operate such a board only if he agreed to purchase all the requisite safety equipment as well, and to follow whatever safety rules we might decide to hand down about the board's use.

In other words, we retained control of his use of the board without agreeing to pay for it. Did our behavior contradict everything else I've said so far about control?

No, because the purchase was totally discretionary; my wife and I merely reminded our son that he had to comply with family rules regarding the ownership and safe operation of inherently dangerous recreational equipment (Owen Family Rule 204-11c). My wife and I made it clear that we considered the cost of the safety equipment to be an indivisible part of the cost of the board. Whether or not he made the (total) expenditure was up to him; how he was allowed to use the thing was up to us.

- *Carelessness and mischief:* My wife and I paid for our kids' school clothes, but if either kid carelessly ruined or lost a sweater or a pair of shoes, paying for the replacement was his or her responsibility, and was not optional. Obviously, leeway has to be given for normal wear-and-tear—and even, I think, for certain kinds of

essentially unavoidable neglect (e.g., leaky pens).
But the financial consequences of truly inconsiderate behavior ought to be the responsibility
of the perpetrator, no matter who made the
purchase in the first place.

- *Upgrades:* You are prepared to spend thirty dollars for a new backpack for your son's school
books; he wants one that costs fifty dollars, but
he hasn't been able to persuade you that it's a
necessity. Should he be allowed to pay the difference and have the backpack he wants?

Sure. That's a good use for a kid's personal
resources. You pay what you would have paid
anyway, while he gets what he wants at what
seems, to him, to be a reasonable price. (If the
more expensive bag looks shoddy or is otherwise something you don't approve of, can you
refuse the bargain? Of course. You don't have to
spend *your* money for something that *you* don't
think is worth the price.)

SHOULD CHILDREN BE ENCOURAGED TO EARN MONEY OUTSIDE THE HOME?

Teenagers are often eager to hold after-school jobs—five million American teenagers currently do so—and their parents often encourage them. Teenagers' social lives can be expensive, and parents generally feel relieved when their kids demonstrate an inclination to take financial responsibility. In addition, parents often feel that the initiative associated with seeking and holding a real job is just exactly what their kids need, from the standpoint of personal growth. Corporate executives, in their ghost-written autobiographies, often attribute at least part of their adult success to the discipline they acquired, after school, as newspaper deliverers, grocery-store baggers, filling-station attendants, and the like. (Oddly, though, they seldom seem to have acquired enough discipline to write their own books all by themselves. Why is that?)

I think such feelings are usually misguided. I believe that unless a family's financial situation forces all hands to contribute, children should not be allowed to hold regular jobs outside of school during the school year. I'm unbothered by occasional, flexible moneymaking opportunities—like weekend baby-sitting assignments, say, or intermittent weekend caddying jobs, or the aforementioned cleaning of the dog run—but I think that true steady employment for high-school students is almost always a mistake.

The main reason for prohibiting children from holding regular after-school jobs can be stated in roughly economic terms: A child's waking hours are limited, and the most profitable place to invest them, both short term and long term, is in education, broadly conceived. I would much rather have found one of my teenaged children, after school, lying on the couch and reading a book than taking orders from the drive-through window at Wendy's. All the virtues that children supposedly acquire from holding menial after-school jobs (punctuality, responsibility, stick-to-itiveness, satisfaction in a job well done) can be acquired just as readily, and far more profitably and enjoyably, at school. Acting in a play, taking photographs for the yearbook, playing on a team, or studying for a test will have a bigger influence on a kid's adult character than will pumping gas or bagging groceries.

In my own case, working on school publications actually turned out to be pretty good preparation for my grown-up career. As a teenager, I never could have found a paying job that provided as much genuine on-the-job training as did editing various school publications or writing a regular newspaper column. So my main extracurricular activities, though unpaid, made a real long-term financial contribution to my life. They were also fun, and they constituted an important part of my adolescent social life.

Bad jobs are mentally exhausting. How sharp would you have been at work today if you had stayed out till eleven last night making french fries? I know teenagers who work thirty or forty hours a week in addition to going to school. They make lots of money, to be sure, and they drive nice cars, but they can't possibly have enough energy left after work to pay much attention when they're in class. The *New Yorker* cartoonist George Booth once told me that he held a full-time job in a printing shop when he was a high-school student, in rural Missouri, and that he sometimes worked all night and went directly to school from the printing shop without stopping off at home. He taught himself to sleep sitting up with his eyes open, so that he could catch up on his rest in class. For all the good he got from those classes, he might as well have been at home in bed.

Teenagers like jobs because jobs generate income, and income generates stuff. Parents tend to feel proud and impressed when their kids become the actual employees of other adults, but most parents would be less pleased if their kids described the inevitable trade-off in a different way: "I've decided that I would rather have a new stereo and a B in English than my old stereo and an A." That's the bargain that working teenagers are really striking. Does it make any kind of sense, economic or otherwise?

Even if you make after-school employment contingent upon your children's success at maintaining some predetermined grade-point average, the kids are still missing out. If they can bus tables twenty hours a week and still make the honor roll, they aren't taking challenging enough courses, or they aren't auditioning for enough plays. (The only exception, I would say, would be the case of a kid who manages to find an after-school job that complements his or her main academic or extracurricular interest—the way Doogie Howser did.)

If you remain unconvinced that most after-school work experience has little value in the long run, push the argument to its extreme. Imagine two children, one of whom drops out of high school in order to work full-time at McDonald's (and thereby gain the maximum possible character enhancement provided by menial employment), and the other of whom stays in high school, takes Advanced Placement courses, plays field hockey, writes for the literary magazine, and earns good grades. Which child is more likely to grow up to be a content, interesting, disciplined, and prosperous working adult?

Truly taking advantage of all the potential benefits of secondary education—including classroom work, homework, sports, clubs, and extracurricular activities—requires a time commitment that adds up to far more than forty hours a week. Kids who "just" go to school aren't slacking off, as long as they're making a reasonably conscientious effort to take advantage of those once-in-a-lifetime opportunities. No student who has a job that consumes forty, thirty, twenty, or even ten hours a week in addition to going to school can possibly be receiving the fullest possible benefit from his or her education. A student who forgoes a chance to play varsity soccer in order to take a financially unnecessary after-school job at 7-Eleven is making a poor trade.

Kids who work long hours after school are also usually giving up what turns out to be, for many people, the most memorable single component of adolescence: the amorphous but emotionally all-consuming social life of the average teenager. Hanging out with friends, going on dates, endlessly talking on the telephone, and instant-messaging late into the night should not be considered frivolous luxuries: they're a big part of what adolescence is all about. When grown-ups think back longingly about their teenage years, those are the kinds of things that bring tears to their eyes. Why allow your kids to deny themselves the same old-fogeyish joys?

Some kids, for financial reasons, have no choice but to work after school. And some kids really do benefit, personally, from having to bear the considerable responsibility of dealing with a real job. But many kids who now work after school don't have to, and, furthermore, the vast majority of them would be better off in the long run if they didn't, or if they worked less. (More than half of American teenagers between the ages of sixteen and nineteen are employed during any given week—a much higher percentage than in most other countries.) If you can afford the luxury of supporting jobless high school students in your home during the school year, you should insist on it—while also insisting, of course, that they not spend all those rescued hours watching TV. Teenagers should be required, if at all possible, to postpone employment until the summer, or, at the very least, until the weekend. That will still leave them plenty of time to learn everything that can be learned from waiting on tables—including the most important lesson of all, which is that waiting on tables is not a great way to make a living.

If Kids Shouldn't Work After School, Who Pays for Their Gas?

Good question. Before I answer it, let's talk about driving.

The life of a family changes forever when a child turns sixteen. The moment I got my driver's license—humiliatingly, on the second try—I was transformed from an annoying but essentially harmless follower of mindless fads into a lethal threat to myself and my community. I didn't notice that change, but my parents must have freaked out. I know, at any rate, that I freaked out when my daughter got her driver's license. (My sister freaked out early. A couple of days after her first son was born, she suddenly burst into tears while rocking him to sleep, because she had just realized that he would one day be old enough to drive. If she had known then that he'd eventually also be old enough buy a rifle at Kmart and have a tattoo on his shoulder, she might have fallen to the floor.)

When children begin to drive, their parents' first thoughts, naturally, concern safety. But their second or third thoughts inevitably concern money. Who's going to pay for all this new driving? What about the insurance? Do you know what gasoline costs? Where did that dent come from? And so forth.

All these issues are emotionally fraught. Let's try to neutralize some of them by adopting a coldly economic perspective.

When teenagers begin to drive, some family costs immediately go up—insurance premiums, fuel charges, body-shop bills—but others typically go down. For example, before my daughter got her driver's license, my kids rode to school on a bus, a service for which I paid a hefty fee. As soon as my daughter could drive, though, she took over the commute, and I stopped paying the fee for her and her brother—a savings for me, even after I subtracted my increased expenses for fuel and depreciation. Even better, my daughter was now available to drive herself and her brother home from after-school play rehearsals and athletic practices, for which bus service had never been available, thereby sparing my wife and me many, many hours of driving. Since my wife and I both work at home, all that saved time made a direct economic contribution to our family: free hours! Our daughter was also now available to take over other driving chores, which we had once had little choice but to perform in her behalf, such as ferrying her to and from the mall or the houses of her friends or her guitar lessons. She even volunteered cheerfully to do many miscellaneous car-related chores from which she gained no personal benefit, and to do quite a bit of driving for her younger brother.

Most of the family economic benefits just described had to be pointed out to me by my daughter, who was making a case, shortly after receiving her driver's license, that I ought to buy all her gas. I strongly disagreed at first—aren't good parents supposed to be angry about how much their children's driving is going to cost them?—but then the undeniable logic of her argument sank in. If my daughter for some reason decided to tear up her driver's license, I asked myself, would I be financially better off or worse off? With her help, I realized that I would be worse off. Knocked off my feet by her icy rationality, I agreed to pay for all her gas. (I also felt proud that she had made an economic case, rather than an emotional one, for why I ought to give her more money.)

It is unfair (and unwise) for parents to focus only on the cost of maintaining a teenaged driver without acknowledging that, in most cases, expanding the family motor pool has significant benefits for the rest of the family, too. The benefits in our family were substantial, as our son (who was thirteen) quickly realized: "When she goes to college, I'm going to be in serious trouble."

Now, Back to Safety

In any family with young drivers, the most important car-related issue is not money, of course; it's safety. But safety has economic implications, too. Safe drivers are much less expensive to maintain than unsafe drivers, because the cost of insuring them is lower, and they don't cause as many trips to the body shop. Does it make sense to offer teenaged drivers an economic incentive for remaining safe?

I think it does. One idea: a safe-driving allowance bonus for every quarter of a year during which a young driver has no moving violations, accidents, insurance claims, or disturbing failures of automotive judgment (as determined by the parents). Here's what you tell your child: if you maintain a good driving record, our family will save money, and to encourage you to do that, I want to share the savings with you.

Why a quarterly bonus instead of a yearly one? I think a year seems so long to a sixteen-year-old that an annual incentive might feel out of reach from the start. And paying up quarterly allows you to reinforce good behavior four times a year instead of just once. It also gives a new driver an additional incentive for refocusing after having the inevitable early-career fender bender—a useful type of accident, in my opinion, because it reminds cocky teenagers that they don't know everything, after all, and that they need to pay more attention when behind the wheel than they may think they do, without threatening their lives.

Incentives usually work better than penalties, and, in addition, they are often easier to administer. If, in contrast, you make your children financially responsible for all their car-related mishaps, the threatened punishment is credible only if the kids have enough money to cover the cost of all the trouble they might get into. A more effective way to punish careless driving episodes, or other examples of undesirable behavior, is to withdraw personal driving privileges for some appropriate period of time, or to require a refresher course of driver education. Many sixteen-year-olds view their driver's license as their most valuable possession; you can take advantage of that fact.

Nevertheless, you have to be careful when you hand out punishments like this—as some friends of mine once discovered, under circumstances that they spent a long time trying to sort out. Their seventeen-year-old son had a minor accident, and they told him that he would not be allowed to drive again until he had paid for the damage to the car. Fine, he said; I'll stop driving. And he did. As a result, his parents then had to take him everywhere he used to take himself, including to and from school every day (twenty-five minutes each way), and he was no longer available to serve as a chauffeur for his younger brother. Because the punishment was open-ended, there was no way that the parents could back down without appearing to have been beaten at their own game. Meanwhile, their son probably figured he could hold out for a few more months, when he would head off to college and be beyond the need of a car.

My friends, in their own self-interest, should at least have separated the two punishments: your license is suspended for (let's say) a month *and* you have to pay for the damage to the car (through regular deductions from your allowance). They weren't prepared for the possibility that their son might decide that his ability to drive was worth less to him, monetarily, than it was to them. (If I were his parents, I think I would decide right away that the time had come to have a big, screaming fight.)

AFTER THE BANK OF DAD

When my daughter was twelve, she told me that she wanted a real checking account of her own. She said she would miss the high rate of return she had received on her account in the Bank of Dad, but that she needed more independence. We negotiated a larger allowance (to make up for the fact that she would no longer be earning 3 percent a month on her account*) and I took her to the bank so that she could sign the forms and pick out checks. I arranged to have her allowance automatically transferred each month from my account to hers. And we signed her up for an ATM card, which was also a MasterCard debit card. When my son was twelve, I did the same thing with him.

Too much responsibility for a seventh-grader? Hardly. Some parents are horrified by the thought of permitting

---

*The major drawback of a regular checking account is that it pays no interest (or a negligible amount of interest) and therefore doesn't encourage saving. In Chapter 6, I'll explain how we solved that problem.

a preteen to carry a debit card, but I think it's a great idea. With a debit card, a kid can buy clothes at Abercrombie & Fitch or order books from Amazon.com, but she can't get into the sort of financial trouble that grown-ups get into with credit cards, because she can't spend more money than she has on deposit. Because all debit-card purchases are recorded on the bank's monthly statement, you can make sure (by snooping) that she isn't buying things you don't want her to buy, or subscribing to Internet services that you wish she didn't even know about. (Make it clear to your kids when you sign them up that you retain the right to inspect their statements whenever you want; depending on the ages of your kids, your bank may even require your name to be on the accounts, too.)

Many young people acquire their first credit cards when they go off to college, after being bombarded with come-ons from card-issuers eager to sign up happy-go-lucky customers. Unless your kids have been prepared properly ahead of time, they may not realize that credit-card interest rates are usually gargantuan, and that balances can get out of hand in a hurry and then keep getting further and further out of hand—something that an astonishing number of supposedly sensible grown-ups don't seem to realize, either. If your kids have had several years' worth of practice with plastic before going off to school, they'll be far less likely to get into trouble. In fact, at some point while they're still under your roof, you may want to move them up from a debit card to a real credit card (with a low credit limit), so that they can get some practice with the temptations of debt while you're still on hand to glare at them meaningfully when they go overboard.

Partly with that in mind, I've encouraged my kids to use their checks or debit cards to pay for purchases that we all view as my responsibility—textbooks, college application fees, school photos—and then bill me for what they spent. Leaving the accounting and paperwork to them encourages them to take a proprietary view of important events in their own lives (such as signing up for the SAT), even if we all know that I'm the one who's ultimately going to pay. If an important deadline comes and goes, they can't blame me for not sending in the check, because they know they could have done so themselves and settled with me later. Besides, kids have better memories than grown-ups do.

Gradually shifting manageable responsibilities from parents to kids is a good idea in any case, and is terrific preparation for adulthood. Tiger Woods's parents did something similar with him when he was growing up. When young Tiger and his father traveled to junior golf tournaments in other cities, for example, Tiger was gradually given responsibility for making their hotel reservations and other travel arrangements, beginning when he was quite young. And when he and his father were on the road together, they would sometimes switch roles, making Tiger the one to decide when they would wake up, when they would leave for the golf course, where they would eat, and so on. Tiger's father was on hand to pick up the pieces if adult-sized problems arose, but Tiger got plenty of real practice at handling the kinds of boring but important duties that he and his father both knew he would soon be handling on his own. The Woodses' example is one that most families could copy profitably in at least a few areas. The idea is not to overwhelm your kids with tasks they aren't yet capable of managing, but to let them gradually become accustomed to some of the unavoidable obligations of adulthood. If you give them the right kind of practice, they'll feel far more prepared and confident when the time comes for them to take over on their own.

5

BEANIE BABY ECONOMICS

WHEN MY SON WAS IN FOURTH GRADE, he and his classmates became temporarily obsessed with collecting the wildly popular plush stuffed animals called Beanie Babies. This mania was widely shared, and it was so powerful that our local toy store would sell out each new shipment within an hour or so of its arrival. My son would buy new Beanies one or two at a time, for about six dollars apiece, whenever he was in funds. He also received Beanies as gifts from relatives and friends. Eventually, he accumulated several dozen.

The girls in my son's class thought of their Beanie Babies mainly as adorable miniature companions. The boys, in contrast, viewed theirs as speculative investments. My son and his friends would study published price guides and the postings in on-line collectors' forums, then cackle as they considered the fortunes they were silently amassing under their beds—although they would sometimes also dump their Beanies down the stairs or take them outside and attempt to throw them over the house.

Whenever I overheard the boys boasting about how much their collections were worth, I performed my fiduciary duty as a gloomy adult by explaining that, notwithstanding whatever expert advice they might have received, Beanie Babies were not scarce and, therefore, couldn't possibly be valuable. I reminded them of the law of supply and demand, and I described how free markets work. "Enjoy your Beanies as projectiles, boys," I said, "but I can promise you that half a dozen nine-year-olds are not going to overturn the laws of economics."

My son ignored me, and, one day, he told me that he needed to raise some cash and had therefore decided to sell two of his "rarest" Beanie Babies, by offering them for sale on eBay, the Internet auction site. I was delighted, since he would now perforce learn an important economics lesson on his own, with no further sermonizing from me. I insisted on editing the wording of his eBay listing—persuading him, for example, that he could not reasonably describe the condition of these toys, which were two years old and had seen hard use both inside and outside our house, as "mint"—and then stepped aside.

Imagine my surprise when, seven days later, the pair sold for $123.50. I helped my son box up his Beanies, warning him not to be disappointed if the buyer, after examining the merchandise, angrily demanded her money back (as I was pretty sure would happen). Imagine my further surprise when, a few days after that, the buyer sent my son an effusive email, saying she was thrilled with her purchase.

End result: I promised my son that I would never again offer him unsolicited advice on any subject whatsoever—although I did suggest that he might want to quickly unload the rest of his collection.

LEARNING FROM eBAY

After recovering from my shock at my son's eBay windfall, I realized that his Beanie Baby experience had presented a far more interesting lesson in economics than the one that I had tried to give him earlier, when I harangued him and his friends about the law of supply and demand. eBay had made it possible for my son to participate in the intoxicating manic phase of a classic speculative bubble—one whose psychological dimensions were exactly like those of the Tulip Mania of seventeenth-century Holland or the South Sea Bubble of eighteenth-century England. Large numbers of seemingly semirational people were buying Beanie Babies only because they knew that large numbers of *other* seemingly semirational people were buying Beanie Babies—and, since it is human nature to assume that almost anyone else knows more than oneself, they were buying them in a state of near-hysterical agitation. By selling part of his collection at what would later turn out to have been the pinnacle of the market's foolishness, my son had made big bucks.

Even better, a few months later, when the crazy prices for Beanie Babies suddenly collapsed, my son completed his education in speculation, by watching the value of his remaining collection drop through the floor—the nation's supply of suckers, despite appearances, always turns out to be finite—while he sat tight. Over a brief period of time, in other words, eBay had enabled my son to learn precisely the same hard facts about hysteria and greed that many adults would later learn far more painfully, after loading up their retirement accounts with Internet stocks and then watching their savings implode.

eBay and Free Enterprise

Such a lesson would not have been readily available to my son in the pre-eBay world. The nature of that world was perfectly captured by the financial writer Andrew Tobias in an anecdote in his book *The Only Investment Guide You'll Ever Need,* which was first published in 1978. When Tobias was a child (he relates in an early chapter) he gradually built a large collection of first-day covers, which are commemorative envelopes bearing brand-new stamps that were postmarked on their day of issue. Coming across his collection many years later, he assumed that it must have become quite valuable, and he decided to sell it. He called a serious stamp collector and asked if the collector would be interested in making an offer.

"How much does your collection weigh?" the collector asked.

Tobias was surprised by the question, but he said that his collection probably weighed "a few pounds."

In that case, the collector said, he would be willing to pay Tobias twenty-five dollars for it. Tobias was amazed— not only because the offered price was far less than the total investment he had made in his collection in the first place, several decades before, but also because the buyer hadn't asked him anything else about his collection, such as what sort of stamps it contained. No doubt feeling at least slightly insulted, he checked with other dealers, looking for a better offer. But he received none. He ended up realizing, sadly, that twenty-five dollars was "not an unfair price."

Tobias's main point was that hoarding stamps, coins, commemorative medallions, baseball cards, or other common "collectibles" was a slow way to get rich. The price you pay to a dealer is almost always vastly higher than the price any dealer would be willing to pay to you for the same item, even many years later. That means that any such investment plunges in value the moment it becomes yours. And while you wait, year after year, for your fortune to arrive, you incur costs for storage and maintenance, and you don't earn interest, dividends, or rent.

Those were the points that Tobias made in his book, and they were essentially the same points that I tried to get across to my son and his friends when I told them that their Beanie Babies were worthless. (In fact, I told them Tobias's story about weighing his stamp collection.) But—as my son's subsequent experience made me realize—the Internet has changed all of that. If Tobias were to sell his stamp collection today, on eBay, he would almost certainly receive a large multiple of the price that he was offered by that pre-Internet collector. Why? Because he would be able to sell his covers directly to amateur buyers like himself, without a professional dealer acting as the intermediary. He would also be able to offer his covers individually, rather than lumping them all together in a single weighable pile, thereby increasing the likelihood that collectors with specialized interests would find, and bid on, items of particular interest to themselves.

He would be able to do that because, in the years since he first attempted to sell his collection, eBay has turned the market for first-day covers and other collectibles, including Beanie Babies, into a true free market, just like the market for cars or the one for personal computers or the one for fast-food meals. Today, because of the Internet, the market for household junk is large enough to operate according to many of the same timeless principles and patterns of behavior that are evident in the commercial world at large. eBay is a microcosm of our total economy.

That makes eBay a terrifically useful economics home laboratory. Internet auctions shrink real free enterprise down to a manageable size, and they pose virtually no barriers to entry. (You don't have to rent retail space or hire employees or even buy a newspaper classified ad to take part.) As a consequence, eBay enables ordinary people, even children, to engage in real commerce with real people from all over the country, and it permits them to do so from the comfort and safety of their own homes. If you are willing to think creatively about buying and selling, and if the Internet doesn't scare you to death,* you and your kids can use eBay to acquire a real, hands-on education in some of the basic principles of free-market economics—something that isn't possible with lemonade stands.

Thanks to eBay, my son and I both gained genuine insight into the behavior of buyers and sellers of all kinds, including, of course, ourselves. We also learned about psychology, marketing, advertising, cost control, responsibility, trust, duplicity, skepticism, irrational exuberance, and idiocy—all valuable economic lessons with lifelong applications far beyond the world of online auctions.

BUYERS' REMORSE

My own first experience with eBay was as a buyer, not a seller. For a brief period, I became a maniacally enthusiastic bidder for the kind of merchandise that used to be

---

*Of course, it's entirely possible that your children already know more about Internet commerce than you do. The teenage son of a friend currently earns a comfortable income by selling illegal copies of bootlegged music recordings to strangers with scary-sounding email addresses. His parents sort of understand what he's up to and are sort of appalled by it, but they are too intimidated by computers to holler at him effectively.

found only in flea markets, garage sales, and curbside trash containers. Most of my purchases were golf-related: a golf-trophy-cum-desk-calendar with an emblem that says "National Amputee"; an old tin practice-ball bucket decorated with a color lithograph of a guy at a driving range; sheet music for a song called "Fore! Ike is on the Tee," copyright © 1953; a ceramic planter shaped like a woman's golf shoe with a golf ball balanced on the toe.

I now regret almost all of those purchases, but they consumed me at the time. My son became similarly deranged, though on a smaller scale. He bought a few old action figures that had been important to him when he was younger, and he bought some old advertising materials related to certain soft drinks that he was fond of, and he bought some used video games. After a couple of months of intermittent buying, though, he made an observation to me which I immediately realized applied to my own experience as well: he said that although his bidding seemed extremely important to him while it was occurring, when an eBay-related package actually arrived for him in the mail, he was often unable to guess what it might contain. In fact, he said, some of his purchases seemed eerily unfamiliar to him even after he had opened the boxes and taken a look. Bidding, for him, had become an end in itself.

This was a useful lesson, and it applied to me as well. Buying of all kinds has a fiercely emotional aspect, especially when the price isn't fixed. Bidders in auctions become partisans the moment they begin to bid, and, unless they are able to keep their emotions in check, their bidding can escalate beyond reason, losing any semblance of what was once a direct connection to the item on sale. (For this reason, my son pointed out to me, items with lower starting prices usually end up attracting higher final bids than items with high starting prices.)

Exactly this same psychopathology is evident on a daily basis throughout our economy. As soon as any kind of buyer, for whatever reason, feels an emotional stake in the outcome of a transaction, the role of rationality is reduced. What is the stock market, after all, but a gigantic auction? Stock-market investors must constantly fight an instinctive urge to take their holdings personally—a result of our hopelessly human tendency to anthropomorphize virtually every aspect of our environment, including marketable securities. Stock investors often hang on to longtime holdings far past the time when selling those holdings would have been smart, simply because they have come to feel emotionally attached. This can happen even to investors who, before making a purchase, are easily able to exercise the most ruthless caution as they unsentimentally compare one possible investment with another. As soon as the trade clears, though, those stock certificates start to seem like family.

You can observe the same all-too-human phenomenon in car dealers' showrooms, where the resolve of coolly calculating buyers usually collapses as soon as the buyers permit themselves to become emotionally attached to a particular car. *Consumer Reports* always advises car buyers to concentrate on getting a good deal, rather than pinning their hopes on any particular model or vehicle—good advice that can be terrifically hard to follow. Once you've pictured yourself behind the wheel, letting go of the image can be tough.

I had a closely related experience when my wife and I were trying to decide whether or not to buy the house in which we now live. I felt deeply ambivalent about the purchase, out of fear that we were making a terrible mistake—until another potential buyer emerged, at which point I immediately began to think of the house as *my* house, and to feel outraged that someone else was trying to take it away from me. This is exactly what bidders in eBay auctions tend to do, and it is the reason why bidders sometimes end up paying more for (let's say) a used golf club than they would have had to pay for a new one.

As it turned out, the other potential house buyer soon disappeared, and I recognized the folly of my reaction. (My wife and I bought the house anyway, and we've lived in it happily for more than fifteen years.) My son, thanks to eBay, gained the very same psychological insight over the course of a few months—and he did so far less traumatically, and at no risk of bankrupting himself and his family. That was a good lesson to learn, and you can help your children learn it, too (or maybe they can help you).

Sellers' Delight

Selling most kinds of items on eBay struck me, initially, as too labor intensive to be worth the trouble: who has the time to do all that posting and checking and waiting and packing and shipping—all in order to sell some lousy trinket for a couple of bucks? One day when I was avoiding work in my office, however, I noticed an unused printing cartridge, which I had bought, a couple of years before, for a laser printer that I now no longer owned. I had paid a lot for the cartridge—more than a hundred dollars—but I had no use for it. I didn't know anyone else who owned the same model of printer. I couldn't take the cartridge back to the store, and, in fact, I wasn't sure where I had bought it. Yet I hated the idea of simply throwing it away. What to do?

Suddenly, I thought of eBay. I listed my cartridge for sale and, a couple of weeks later, received a check for eighty bucks (including shipping). I stuck stamps and a mailing label directly on the cartridge's unopened box and took it to the post office. That was that. The buyer came out ahead, because he received a perfectly good cartridge for thirty bucks less than Staples would have charged him. And I came out ahead, even given the highly unrealistic rate at which I calculate the value of my time. The experience was a revelation for me. Suddenly, a lot of the junk lying around my house stopped looking like junk and started looking like money.

My son had a similar experience at around the same time. He bought a new video game for himself and was surprised to discover that, as a result of some fortuitous manufacturing screwup, the box contained two copies of the game disk rather than just one. He quickly realized that the manufacturer's error offered him an opportunity to recoup most of his cost. Keeping one of the disks for his own use, he offered the other for sale on eBay (along with the box and all the supporting documentation), and soon sold it for very nearly as much as he had paid for the game in the first place—money that he immediately invested in another video game.

This experience had the same effect on him that selling my old printer cartridge had on me: it opened his eyes to the cash value of the junk cluttering his room. He quickly sold off a substantial portion of his private cache of old video games, unwanted CDs, and outgrown toys. His previously vague sense of the value of his possessions was transformed. Later, when he bought new video games, he saved all the original packaging, so that he could create the most appealing possible presentation later on, when he resold the game on eBay after (inevitably) becoming bored with it. He also handled all his current games carefully and put them away when he wasn't using them, because he knew that their resale value would drop if he didn't.

This is so important, it's worth repeating. One of the most valuable lifelong financial services that you can perform for your children, I believe, is to help them begin to think of themselves as the owners of their lives, rather than renters or squatters—in other words, to help them begin to take personal responsibility in the broadest possible sense. eBay, by providing an accessible and convenient marketplace in which things like old CDs and video games have genuine monetary value, has transformed my son's relationship to his possessions. By giving him an incentive for behaving responsibly, eBay has increased his personal sense of responsibility. That's good!

GREED, OPPORTUNISM, AND STUPIDITY

One of eBay's greatest contributions is providing an accessible forum where one can conveniently observe greed, opportunism, and stupidity in action. On September 11, 2001, the day terrorists destroyed the World Trade

Center and attacked the Pentagon, I watched the unfolding story on television in horror and with a steadily deepening sense of dread, as we all did. At some point during that terrible morning, though, I suddenly wondered (in my capacity as a staff writer for a weekly magazine) what effect the tragedy had had on the market for World Trade Center memorabilia on eBay.

Around lunchtime, the offerings began to swell. Posters, T-shirts, prints, drawings, paperweights, postcards, pens, and shot glasses—the kind of junk that any tourist could have bought by the truckload from sidewalk vendors all over Manhattan just a few hours before—came onto the market throughout the afternoon. Most of those items found bidders immediately, often for prices that quickly rose into the hundreds of dollars.

The bidders were bidding because they believed that the destruction of the World Trade Center had made World Trade Center souvenirs suddenly scarce, and therefore valuable. But of course this was a misconception. It was the World Trade Center itself that had become scarce, not the souvenirs—millions of which had been sold to tourists over the previous twenty-five years, and millions more of which could be manufactured easily.

The attempt to exploit tragedy for gain was appalling, of course. But there was also something at least slightly reassuring about those auctions: not giving a sucker an even break is about as American as you can get, and that part of our culture, at least, was still fully intact.* My son and I both marveled at the muddled thinking of the bidders. They had acted exactly like the benighted investors who bid up the prices of essentially worthless dot-com shares during the final months of the great Internet stock bubble, because they mistook the top of the market for the bottom and were afraid of missing out.

As luck would have it, the stock market is the main subject of the very next chapter.

---

*A few weeks later, my son read in the newspaper that people all over the country were buying all the gas masks they could find, because they were worried about the possibility of chemical or biological attacks by terrorists. He remembered that he himself owned an old gas mask, which he had bought for a few dollars at a military-surplus store a couple of years before, to use as a prop in a sixth-grade science-class presentation on the Ebola virus. He offered the gas mask for sale on eBay, and, within a couple of hours, had sold it for seventy dollars.

6

The Dad Stock Exchange

ONE OF THE MOST USEFUL SERVICES that we can perform as parents is to provide our kids with opportunities to screw up in interesting ways that make lasting impressions but do no genuine harm. We all learn mainly by trial and error, and our most important insights often arise from our biggest mistakes.

When it comes to investing, I think, kids should be allowed to begin screwing up as early as possible, because many of the truly valuable lessons take years to sink in. An investor whose knowledge of the stock market consisted solely of what happened to American equities between 1995 and 1999, for example, would have a very different view from that of an investor who knew only what happened between 1999 and today. Ideally, a young investor's education should include both of those kinds of experiences, and many others besides. The best way to be sure that happens is to start early.

Starting early is tricky, though. Stocks and bonds are harder to understand than savings accounts are. That means that parents have to be prepared to do more explaining, and kids have to be interested in hearing the explanations. In addition, kids can gain meaningful experience only if they truly participate. That is, they have to risk money of their own. Some of the most valuable investment lessons have to do with understanding what happens to investors' sense of judgment as their net worth rises and falls. That sense of judgment is heavily influenced by many noneconomic factors, among them greed, panic, fear, envy, shame, adrenaline, and ego. Your kids won't really feel those influences unless the stakes are real.

THE PROBLEM

That creates a problem. You can't let young kids make real buy-and-sell decisions in the real stock market, for several reasons: minors can't legally own stocks in their own names without adults serving as custodians; your kids' investing mistakes, though possibly instructive to them from an educational point of view, could be devastating to them or to your family from a financial point of view; making allowance-sized purchases and sales of real equities would subject your kids to prohibitively high brokerage commissions and other expenses, which, even at the low rates charged by Internet-only brokerages, would have a devastating effect on any gains they might realize, by nullifying years' worth of profits. (Even paying a commission of just a dollar per trade would ruin the performance of an investor moving ten or twenty dollars at a time.)

One popular alternative is to let children make fantasy or imaginary investments. There are many "virtual stock markets" or simulated stock-investing games available on the Internet and elsewhere, and the financial-news television network CNBC runs a well-known stock-picking tournament for high-school students—or, at any rate, it used to run such a tournament back in the days when stocks went only up. My daughter's history class did something similar when she was in seventh or eighth grade. The teacher required each kid to pick one real stock to research and follow over the course of the term, and most of the kids enjoyed the experience.

But all such exercises have little true educational value. The participants, with no money at stake, don't truly care what happens to their "investments." They aren't risking anything of their own, so their emotional involvement is low. I suppose my daughter's teacher could have made his stock exercise more realistic by basing the kids' history grades solely on the performance of their stock picks, but the kids (and their parents) would have had a cow about that one.

Besides, following a single stock over a single semester yields results that are meaningless in the long run and, therefore, can only be misleading. School stock-picking projects may help kids learn how to read the stock pages of a newspaper and how to search for investing information on the Internet, but they can't do much else. Teaching kids about the stock market by requiring them to follow one stock for three months is like teaching them about literature by having them read one page from the middle of one book.

Similarly, stock-picking tournaments like the one on CNBC really do nothing except to encourage reckless investing behavior, because they impose no penalty for being wrong. Students who participate in stock-picking contests quickly realize that the only way to have a chance of winning is to concentrate exclusively on highly volatile, highly speculative investments—because those are the only kinds of investments that are likely to make huge moves in short periods of time. The most sensible strategy in such a tournament is always to favor the very riskiest securities, because those are, generally speaking, the only ones whose prices have any chance of going up by a gigantic percentage before the tournament ends. If the stocks go down by a gigantic percentage instead, so what? You can always try again, with a different selection of extremely risky stocks, the following week.

Making fantasy investments is like playing poker with chips that have no cash value: the most important element of the activity is missing. The essence of both poker and investing lies in what happens to the minds of the participants when things are going well and when things are going poorly.

A Solution

The only possible solution, I eventually decided, was to start a stock market of my own. Doing that turned out to be even easier than starting the Bank of Dad, and I think you should consider starting one for your kids, too— although there are several serious complications involved in offering both a bank and a brokerage at the same time, as I will explain later in this chapter.

The stock market I created was called the Dad Stock Exchange. To handle my kids' investments, I created an investment firm called Dad & Co., which resided on my computer, just as the Bank of Dad once did. As I did with my bank, I used Quicken to keep track of my kids' accounts.

The stocks in my exchange were imaginary in the sense that they existed only in my records—so the Securities and Exchange Commission had no authority over them, and trading them had no tax implications—but my stocks were just like real stocks in almost every other way. Their prices rose and fell in perfect lockstep with those of real stocks. My kids paid real money when they bought them, and they received real money when they sold. If they bought low and sold high, they made real profits; if they bought high and sold low, they incurred real losses. I myself acted as the all-powerful market maker in all transactions—which is to say that I took the other side of every trade. When my kids bought stocks, they were really buying them only from me; when they sold stocks, they were really selling them back.

The prices of the securities traded on my exchange corresponded exactly to the prices of real securities, with one important exception: the securities on my exchange were denominated in pennies rather than in dollars. Thus, on a day when a single share of IBM on the New York Stock Exchange traded for $95, a single share of IBM on the Dad Stock Exchange traded for 95 cents, exactly one one-hundredth as much. On the same day, a hundred shares of McDonald's could have been had for $28.50 on my stock exchange, or exactly the same price as a single share of McDonald's on Wall Street.

Denominating shares in pennies rather than dollars was useful, I believe, because it knocked prices down to levels that were appropriate and manageable for investors whose main income source was an allowance, while maintaining an exact and obvious relationship with the real world. My kids could easily track the value of their holdings in the same way I track the value of mine: by checking the Internet or the television or the newspaper. They just had to remember to move every decimal point two places to the left. For example, when the newspaper reported that Intel closed yesterday at 22.50—or when Quicken, via the Internet, updated Intel's most recent price per share to 22.50—my kids thought simply "cents" instead of "dollars." No other conversion is necessary.

I could have accomplished much the same thing by permitting my kids to buy and sell small fractions of shares, based on their actual stock-market prices. But I think denominating in pennies made everything easier for all of us to keep track of; it involved far less confusing arithmetic, because off-the-shelf financial software continued to work without modification. Let's say, for example, that my son had a ten-dollar bill burning a hole in his pocket, and he wanted to use that money to buy stock in Chevron Corp.—which, at the moment, was trading for $87.11 a share on the New York Stock Exchange. On the

Dad Stock Exchange, where Chevron was, therefore, trading for a little more than 87 cents a share—$0.8711, to be precise—he could buy 11 shares (and receive 42 cents in change); if I had dealt in fractional shares instead, I would have had to credit him for 0.114 of a share, and many financial software packages wouldn't have even recognized the transaction. Letting dollars stand for pennies kept everything easy to follow and easy to understand.

STARTING A STOCK EXCHANGE OF YOUR OWN

When I was first planning Dad & Co., I considered simply creating some ground rules and inviting my kids to invest as much or as little of their own money as they might like. Eventually, though, I realized that such an open-ended offer might very well seem overwhelming (or beside the point) to them. Roughly three thousand stocks are listed on the New York Stock Exchange alone, after all, and thousands more are traded on the NASDAQ Stock Market, and thousands upon thousands of other possible investments are available in various corners of the economy. A better idea, I decided, would be to pick a few stocks myself—ones with names I knew my kids would recognize—and thereby give them a narrow focus for their first investment decisions. They wouldn't have to sort through the entire universe of possible investments; they would merely have to decide for themselves whether or not their father's initial picks stunk. And even if the kids did nothing, they would still have portfolios, which curiosity alone would almost certainly prompt them to keep an eye on from time to time.

I picked six stocks for my kids: Intel (the brains in their computers), Microsoft (the software in their computers), Nokia (the source of their cell phones), AOL (the principal medium through which they communicate with their friends), McDonald's (sustenance), and the Gap (clothes). I told my kids that I had chosen these particular stocks not because I had feelings about them one way or another as investments, but because I knew that the kids were familiar with the names and the products. I announced what I had done in a letter that contained the following:

1. With some money given to you by Grammie and Pa, I have opened an account for you in my new brokerage firm, which is called Dad & Co. To get you started, I've created a portfolio for you containing one hundred shares each of six different stocks. At Friday's closing prices, your portfolios were each worth a bit less than $250.

2. Your account belongs to you. You may sell all your stocks, withdraw all your money, and close

your account right now, if you like. Or you may sell some or all of your stocks and buy different ones. Or you may buy additional stocks with money you add to your account. Or you may sell some stocks and keep others and withdraw all the cash. Or you may do nothing. Or you may do anything else you can think of. All profits (or losses) belong to you.

3. To make it easier for you to buy and sell reasonable numbers of shares, all the stocks on my stock exchange will be priced at exactly 1/100th of their actual price at the moment of purchase or sale—that's one penny for every dollar. In other words, a share of stock that costs one hundred and one dollars on the New York Stock Exchange costs one hundred and one cents on the Dad Stock Exchange. Your account at Dad & Co. isn't just for stocks. It also includes a money market account, which is a lot like a savings account but pays a better interest rate. The interest rate on a Dad & Co. money market account is currently half a percent a month, payable on the last day of the month. Compounded monthly, that works out to an annual rate of a little more than six percent. If you have extra cash lying around in your regular checking

account, you can withdraw it and deposit it (by
writing a check to me) in your Dad & Co.
account, where it will earn interest. You can buy
stocks with that money, if you like, or you can
withdraw it at any time for any reason, or you
can leave it alone and let it earn interest for as
long as you like.

4. Through your Dad & Co. account, you can also
invest in any other investment that you and I can
find reliable prices for in the newspaper or
online. You can invest in mutual funds, munici-
pal bonds, pork bellies, crude oil, stock options,
or anything else that you can think of—and I
will be happy to explain what these things are (if
I know) or help us both find out (if I don't).
Like your stocks, all these other types of investments will be priced at Dad & Co. in pennies
instead of dollars. And the decision to buy or sell
them will be yours alone.

5. If you would like to buy or sell something when
I am not around, you can send me your order by
email and I will later enter the trade in your account for the price of the investment at the exact
time your email was sent. Please include that
price in your email. (You can also write your or-

der on a piece of paper and leave it on my desk.) Since you are almost always in school during the hours when the stock market is open, I will allow you to buy and sell after hours at the most recent closing price. I will give you investment advice if you want it (and if you trust my advice), but you can do anything you like with your account, and all your investment decisions are yours.

7. You can easily keep track of the value of your investments by using any of several free services online, including your personalized Excite or Yahoo start page. I will be happy to help you set up a portfolio tracker in either of those, or maybe you can show me a better way to handle mine. Just remember that for our purposes the quoted prices signify pennies rather than dollars.

8. If the stocks you own pay dividends, I will credit those dividends to your account once a year, at the end of December, and I will do it fairly approximately, based on each stock's annual yield, which you can check through any stock-tracking program on the Internet. Most companies distribute their dividends quarterly, but I would go crazy if I tried to do that. If I err, I will do my best to err in your favor.

9. I will keep track of your accounts in Quicken on my computer, and I will print out statements for you periodically, or whenever you ask. (You may need to remind me to add the interest on your money-market balance.) You can also check your accounts on my computer at any time.

LETTING YOUR KIDS TAKE IT FROM THERE

Immediately after reading my letter, my son rearranged his portfolio, throwing out a couple of my picks and adding several new ones of his own (at a cost to himself of some additional cash, which he paid to me by check); my daughter was a little slower to become interested in her account, although soon she, too, rearranged her holdings. She also made a large deposit into her Dad & Co. money market fund, because she was tired of earning nothing on her checking-account balance.

The next year, I made another addition to my kids' Dad & Co. accounts, once again with money that had been given to them for that purpose by their grandparents. This time, though, I made the additions not in individual securities but in three kinds of mutual funds: a corporate-bond index fund, a value-oriented stock fund, and a broad stock index fund. When I did so, I had to explain what mutual funds, bonds, and indexes were.

Not long afterward, my daughter—who had suffered some losses in several of the stocks in her portfolio, including two that she had picked herself—decided that she was no longer interested in owning individual equities at all. She asked me to sell all her individual stocks and to help her choose mutual funds in which to reinvest the proceeds. She said that she was too busy with school to give her investments the time they required, and that she would prefer to leave that job to an assortment of professional fund managers—a very valuable and mature discovery about herself, which she had gained at small cost. (A grown-up friend of mine made exactly the same discovery at the age of fifty, after losing half a million dollars in the stock market in a short period of time with the help of a broker at a major brokerage, the name of which you would recognize in an instant.)

NEUTRALITY

With both my kids, I tried mostly to be a neutral observer rather than a financial adviser. I made a few unsolicited remarks about the stock market, and I commented on a couple of good and bad investments of my own, and I showed them the real portfolios that I managed in their behalf. And I did my best to explain various different kinds of investments.

For the most part, though, I said nothing unless asked. I didn't want my kids to simply reproduce my own successes and failures as an investor; I wanted them to begin to get a feel for investing on their own. I wanted them to see how their wealth was affected by unpredictable global events (such as the terrorist attacks of September 11, 2001) as well as by strictly economic or financial news. My goal was not to impart "wisdom"—which I don't have a surplus of—but to allow them to acquire some firsthand experience at weighing financial risks. It's always hard to learn from other people's mistakes, because you can't help believing that if you had been in their situation, you wouldn't have been as dumb. I thought my kids would learn faster if the mistakes they made were truly their own.

I also tried to avoid the natural adult temptation to spoil an interesting, educational experience by burying it under layers of punitive responsibilities: I didn't charge my kids brokerage commissions, and I didn't tax their capital gains. Trading costs and taxes are a real part of the real investment world, but kids don't need to be burdened with all the sordid details right away. They'll learn all there is to know about taxes and transaction costs soon enough. I figure I taught them plenty by simply giving them some real opportunities to observe their own tolerance for the trade-off between risk and reward.

WHAT ABOUT THE BANK OF DAD?

The Dad Stock Exchange couldn't open for business until the Bank of Dad had shut down. Why? Because no sensible investor would give up a guaranteed interest rate of 3 percent a month—backed by the full faith and credit of Dad himself—in order to invest in the stock market. (Heck, if anyone ever offers you even a guaranteed 1 percent a month, you should sell all your stocks and take it, because 1 percent a month is well above the average return on stocks over the past century or so.)

I fretted about that fact during the years when my kids were still Bank of Dad customers. I wanted them to get some experience with the stock market, but I didn't want to force them to make an investment move that my own banking system had rendered irrational. What to do?

One possibility that occurred to me was to put a ceiling on Bank of Dad account balances, so that the kids would have little choice but to move their excess funds to Dad & Co. once they had hit whatever limit I imposed (say, two hundred or three hundred dollars). But I worried that such a move might seem confusing, and I didn't really want to take away the saving incentive I had gone to such trouble to create. Nor did I want to suggest that a totally risk-free investment (the Bank of Dad) carried far higher average returns than a very risky one (the Dad Stock Exchange).

But my kids solved my problem for me, by deciding, at the age of twelve, that they wanted real checking accounts and real debit cards (see Chapter 4). That pushed the guaranteed return on their savings to zero, thereby making the stock market seem potentially worth the added risk. And by offering them a money market fund, I provided a risk-free savings alternative, in case they decided to chicken out.*

---

*A good way to encourage saving by older kids, instead of paying them monthly interest, is to offer to match their own efforts to save toward some worthy goal—like an employer-matched 401(k) plan at work. The daughter of friends of ours told her father, when she was twelve, that she wanted to be able to buy a car when she was old enough to drive. He told her that he would match her own savings, dollar for dollar, and by the time she was seventeen she had saved enough, from babysitting and other jobs, to buy one. He was, in effect, paying her 100 percent interest on her savings. That boost made her goal achievable, which kept her interested in achieving it.

QUESTIONS TO PREPARE FOR: EXPLAINING
THE STOCK MARKET TO YOUR KIDS

Stock-market investments are harder to understand than savings-account investments are, so if you want to introduce your kids to the stock market, you're going to have to do some explaining. Here's the main question:

What do you really own when you own a share of stock?

This is a question that a parent ought to be prepared to answer—or to ask rhetorically, if the kids don't ask it themselves.

A good answer begins with the one my father gave me when I was a lad: when you own a share of stock, you own a very small but very real piece of the company that issued it. I remember being extraordinarily impressed by that idea, and I can still vaguely hear myself bragging about it to my friends in the first or second grade. One of the small holdings in the custodial account that my father managed in my behalf at that time was a few shares of the stock of Ford Motor Company. As a result, I realized, I owned a little tiny piece of every Ford factory and office building and desk and paper clip and parking lot— all mine, although in many cases my pieces would have had to be measured in molecules, if not electrons. Still, when I saw a light blue 1962 Ford Fairlane driving down the street, I thought, "I *made* that car." I also knew that I, as a partial owner of the company, was entitled to a small piece of Ford's profits, and that my piece of those profits would be paid to me (or, rather, added to my custodial account) in the form of quarterly dividends.

As a Ford stockholder I also owned a third thing, which was often the most important thing of all, although I never thought about it then: I owned a small piece of every positive, negative, neutral, smart, stupid, and crazy opinion that I and everyone else in the world might have about the Ford Motor Company and its stock, and about the future of both. The stock market is a market, just like the market for Beanie Babies, and the price of a share of Ford, at any given moment, is not infallibly determined by some scientific formula based on book value and profits, but is heavily influenced by the fears, hopes, enthusiasms, misconceptions, doubts, expectations, rationalizations, emotions, misunderstandings, irrationalities, dreams, and mental problems of everyone who buys or sells the stock, or gossips about it at a party, or writes about it in the newspaper, or talks about it on TV, or lies about it in an Internet chat room. In other words, the value of a share of stock is ultimately determined by the opinions of human beings. Those opinions may be heavily influenced by paper-and-pencil valuations of the company's assets and by various objective measures of the company's performance as a business, but, in the end, a stock, like a Beanie Baby, is worth what people decide it's worth.

To summarize: when you own a share of stock, you own three things:

- you own a small part of what the company owns;

- you own a small part of what the company earns;

- you own a small part of what other people think about the company and about its stock.

THE SAME THING, ONLY BACKWARD

Another way to explain all this to a child is to approach the matter from the opposite direction, by asking the child to imagine owning not a small piece of a company like Ford but owning the whole thing. If your daughter, for some reason, owned the entire Ford Motor Co., what would she own? Well, she would own all those factories and parking lots and paper clips all by herself. She would also be in charge. She would get to sit at the chairman's desk if she wanted to, or she could hire someone else to sit there for her. She could suddenly decide to stop making trucks, or to sell the company's headquarters and spend the proceeds on candy, or to paint all of next year's Tauruses purple, or to do anything else she wanted to do. And if Ford earned a profit, that profit would be hers alone, since she would be the sole owner of the business. She could store her profit in a gigantic piggy bank, or invest it in a new minivan assembly plant, or use it to buy a chain of pizza restaurants, or whatever.

In reality, of course, Ford has many owners—all the stockholders—not just one. But those stockholders collectively possess all the same powers that your daughter would possess all by herself if she single-handedly owned that great big pile. Ford's many stockholders, acting together, get to make all the same decisions—although they do so indirectly (if they bother even to do that), usually by voting for slates of directors, who make some big decisions themselves but typically choose other people to make other decisions in behalf of all the stockholders.

Stockholders run a company, in other words, in essentially the same way that voters run our country: by choosing other people to handle the dirty work for them. Their ownership is every bit as real as your daughter's would be if she owned the company all by herself; their ownership is just spread among a large group of people, who exercise their powers collectively rather than individually. That's what it means to say that a stockholder really and truly owns a small piece of the company that issued her stock.

Ford's stockholders make, or lose, money in pretty much the same ways that your daughter would if she owned the company all by herself, though they do so less directly. If Ford distributes part of its profits to shareholders in the form of dividends, the shareholders make money by pocketing those; if Ford's business is good, or if its future business prospects look good, they may be able to make money by selling their shares at a profit to other investors, who are willing to pay a good price because they are eager to get in on the act; if Ford's current business is bad, or if its future business prospects look bad, they may lose money by selling their shares to other investors for less than they paid for them in the first place.

WHERE DO STOCKS COME FROM?

One day my son asked me a good question that many adults never think to ask: Where do stocks come from?

The answer is that stocks originally come from the companies themselves, which sell shares to the public in order to raise money. The companies may use that money for a variety of purposes (such as building new factories, paying off debts, or allowing the original owners to retire to a tropical island).

After that initial sale, though, the company doesn't stand to directly gain (or lose) from subsequent sales or purchases of the same shares. If I buy one hundred shares of Ford tomorrow, for example, I will be buying them not from Ford but from some other stockholder, who bought them from someone else, who bought them from someone else, who bought them from someone else, and so on. Ford's only connection to my shares is that my possession of them turns me into a partial owner of the company, and therefore entitles me to dividends, annual reports, a vote at the company's annual meeting, and so on. In other words, my purchase of Ford shares entails a variety of obligations for Ford, but no money.

There are complicated ways in which companies actually are affected by subsequent sales and purchases of their shares, but if your kids are that inquisitive, they're smart enough to pursue the issue on their own and then explain it to you.

What Are Bonds?

When you buy bonds issued by a company, you aren't buying a piece of the company; you're lending the company money. If I buy a thousand dollars' worth of Ford bonds, what I am really doing is lending Ford a thousand dollars for some set period of time. In return, Ford pays me interest at a set rate and promises to return my loan at the end of the period. Bonds are generally safer than stocks as investments, but their returns are generally lower.

You can also buy bonds from entities other than companies. The most important issuer is the United States of America, which sells bonds of one sort or another for periods of between three months and ten years. Why does our government need to borrow money? It needs to borrow money because it usually spends more (on salaries, bombs, dams, and other expenses) than it collects in taxes and other revenues; that's what the federal deficit is. When you buy bonds, you are lending the government the money it needs to cover the national debt. U. S. government bonds are generally known as the safest investments in the world, because they are certain to retain their value for as long as the United States remains in business. Because they are so safe, the interest rate they pay is pretty low.

WHAT IS A MUTUAL FUND?

A mutual fund pools together money from lots of different people and invests the total pool in stocks, bonds, or other securities, or any number of possible combinations. The main appeal of mutual funds is that they enable small investors to spread their money across more different investments than they would be able to if they were instead buying, say, individual stocks. There are lots and lots of different kinds of funds, and you can explain those kinds to your children if they seem interested. Doing so may require you do a little preliminary research of your own—a chore hugely simplified by the Internet.

One problem with offering mutual funds to your children through your own brokerage is that doing so requires you to keep track of, and give your kids credit for, the funds' distributions of dividends and realized capital gains, which usually occur in the fourth quarter of every year. The best way to do that is probably to look for the relevant information on each fund's website at year-end—but you'll have to check and recheck your arithmetic, because the figures can be confusing. You'll definitely need to do it, though, because the changes in value can be significant. If you don't give your kids proper credit for the distributions, their fund investments will appear to be worth less than they are.

7

True Net Worth

Kids often say they hope to be really, really rich, and why shouldn't they? Heated underground swimming pools, jet packs, personal submarines, and mansions equipped with automatic candy dispensers don't come cheap, so if you intend to possess those amenities when you grow up, you'd better be prepared to lay your hands on some serious bucks. Kids who say they want to be billionaires aren't necessarily being greedy; often, they're just being realistic about what they perceive to be their long-term needs.

Maintaining such a pragmatic attitude about wealth becomes harder as the years go by. Grown-ups, too, often say they want to be rich, but their yearning usually lacks the sharp, results-oriented focus that it had when they were young. Adults' ideas about wealth tend to get mixed up with lots of other ideas, many of them muddled or darkly neurotic. Often, adults want to be rich because, well, they've tried everything else. Either that or they have friends who've got more money than they do, and they can't stand to be near them. As the years go by, money can begin to seem less like a useful tool than like a last crack at salvation.

Sorting through such issues is made difficult by the undeniable truth that money, more often than not, really can buy happiness, or at least peace of mind. Having plenty of money instantly alleviates all the worst money-driven conflicts and anxieties—which, for the majority of people, are among the most consistently oppressive burdens of everyday life—thereby freeing up huge chunks of human consciousness for more gratifying uses. Rich people sometimes claim to have been happier when they were poor, but no matter what they or various sages may claim about the true sources of content-ment, people who have enough money sleep better at night than people who don't. It's hard to be a productive member of the human race if your decision not to take your sick child to the doctor arose from your fears about the appointment's probable cost.

These contradictory feelings about money inevitably affect our kids. One of the many great challenges that we face as parents, therefore, is to embody, in the presence of our children, an attitude about monetary wealth which acknowledges its wonderfulness yet doesn't raise absurd expectations or engender weird symbolic dependencies. It is unfair for parents to assert to their children that money and happiness are unrelated, because even preschoolers readily see the connection; at the same time, though, parents must try not to allow their own financial hang-ups to convince their children that money itself is the meaning of life, or of love, or of human fulfillment. This balancing act is hard for everybody, but it's especially difficult for families at the far ends of the spectrum of affluence: both rich parents and poor parents have a tough time raising children who are entirely untraumatized by their net worth.

When I was a young kid, I felt annoyed when grown-ups claimed that the truly rich people in the world were the ones with kind hearts, good health, interesting hobbies, and so forth. There was scattered evidence to support such assertions, but I knew for a fact that I wasn't going to be able to buy my own Aston Martin DB5 with just good table manners and a smile. Later, when I became an aspiring hippie, I felt similarly exasperated by anyone who seemed to think that money meant anything at all (while nonetheless managing to find interesting uses for any dollars that happened to materialize in the pockets of my bell bottoms).

Now that I'm a grown-up, my feelings have become

hopelessly tangled. I love my beautiful, wonderful money and everything it does for me, but I also understand that the most important sources of happiness in my life have seldom been the ones with the highest price tags. Maintaining a reasonably healthy balance between those two attitudes has required emotional and intellectual tinkering on an almost daily basis. Even harder, for me, has been finding ways to communicate some sense of that balance to my kids.

For all these reasons, I think we parents can do an enormous favor for our children (and for ourselves) by making a conscious, ongoing effort to enlarge and complicate the entire family's understanding of wealth. To pull this off, though, we first need to give our own views a thorough examination and updating.

TRUE NET WORTH

Anyone who has ever applied for a large loan, or tried to decide how much life insurance to buy, or been a regular reader of personal-finance magazines, is familiar with the concept of calculating personal net worth. You add up all your assets (bank balances, home equity, stock holdings, the market value of your furniture) and subtract all your liabilities (mortgage balance, car loans, credit-card debt, yet-to-be-paid taxes on capital gains). The resulting figure is your financial liquidation value—the size of the pile of money you'd be left with if you sold all your possessions and investments, and paid off all your creditors.

Knowing your net worth can be indispensable in certain real-life situations, such as planning for retirement or death. But net worth isn't a very useful guide for day-to-day living, because it counts assets only at their market value, which may grossly understate or overstate their real significance to you—and it doesn't count nonfinancial assets, which may be just as important. Well, I've wrestled with this issue for quite a while, and I've come up with a notion that, to me, seems more interesting. I'll call my notion True Net Worth.

Estimating True Net Worth is not a step-by-step process. You won't need a calculator or your most recent brokerage statement—a disappointment, no doubt, if you are one of the many people who get a kick out of filling out financial surveys. In fact, you won't really need to add or subtract much of anything at all. The point of thinking about True Net Worth is not to come up with a number but to discover ways of making small adjustments, here and there, in the way you think about value and, ultimately, in the way you live. Thinking about True Net Worth can also help your children learn to conduct their own lives in ways that may someday help them maximize their own contentment.

What Would You Put in the Box?

On Christmas morning about ten years ago, a small fire broke out in the house of a family my wife and I know. There were cracks in the masonry in their fireplace, and some smoldering embers sifted down into the wood framing near the hearth, and, a couple of hours later, smoke began to rise up through the floor. My friends called 911 and then had to make a nearly instantaneous decision about what, if anything, to carry with them when they evacuated their home. After a split-second's contemplation, they grabbed their family photo albums as they headed for the door.

I've thought about that decision off and on for the past decade, and I haven't come up with a better one. If I had to flee my house in a hurry, I'd ignore jewelry and computers and our big new expensive TV set (which I wouldn't be able to lift anyway, as I know from having thrown my back out by trying to move it on Christmas Eve several years ago), and, instead, I would reach for our own scrapbooks, which, conveniently, reside on a shelf just a few paces from the front door. I'm a semicompulsive photo-album compiler, and the entire set now comprises more than a dozen volumes. Over the years, those volumes have provided innumerable hours of entertainment and comfort for me, my wife, our kids, our relatives, and others. Life without the scrapbooks would seem horribly diminished; if everything else were gone, those scrapbooks would provide an emotional foundation upon which the other members of my family and I would begin to rebuild our lives.*

In that sense, therefore, shouldn't I consider my photo albums to be my most valuable possession—the number one asset in my compilation of my True Net Worth? The albums aren't valuable in a strictly monetary sense; I couldn't sell them to anyone else, even though by this point they represent several thousand dollars' worth of photo-printing expense. Insuring them would be pointless, because no amount of money could bring them back into existence if they vanished in a fire. Their value is purely emotional, and that value, to me and to the other members of my family, is immense.

(What I should do immediately, I suddenly realize, is take my photo albums to some sort of photocopying shop, and have full-sized color copies made of all of them, and then store those copies at my parents' house or some other secure, remote location. I hope I do that soon.)

---

*In case you're wondering, my friends' house didn't burn down after all, although it did sustain some moderately serious damage. I do know another family that really did lose all their possessions in a house fire, though, and they were devastated by the loss. As the husband said a few months later, "After a while, the fact that everybody got out safely no longer seems like enough."

Of roughly equal value to me is a lengthy diary, which I kept for about ten years while my children were little. The diary is a chronicle of my children's early lives, and it focuses mainly on funny things they said or did before they were old enough to know better. ("Dave, is cheese vegetables, or what is it?" my daughter asked me one day when she was four.) Like the scrapbooks, the diary has generated many happy hours of reflection over the years for me and all the members of my family. When I open it randomly and read a few pages, entire lost eras are vividly brought back to life in my mind. I look forward to obsessively reading that diary over and over many years from now, when I'm living out my final days in some nursing home.

What is your most valuable possession—the item or items that ought to be listed at the top of your accounting of your True Net Worth? You probably won't be able to answer off the top of your head, but thinking about how you might answer would be a useful ongoing exercise, as it would for anyone. And if your children are old enough to understand the concept, you can also suggest to them that they might find it interesting to think about the same thing. (If your children are very young, you already know what their most valuable possession is: the blanket, stuffed animal, or beloved toy that would cause you to turn your car around and drive back a hundred miles after leaving for vacation without it.) For older children, the exercise can lead to useful meditations on true value. For example, you might casually ask your children—maybe somewhere near the middle of a long, tedious afternoon toward the end of a school vacation—what they would most want to hang on to if for some reason they had to get rid of everything in their rooms except whatever they could fit into (let's say) a medium-sized cardboard box. What would they decide to keep? You might even give them an actual box and ask them to try it.

This exercise is illuminating because it forces an answerer to separate the concept of value from the concept of cost. Thoughtfully answering the question may suggest, to your children and to yourself, that there are forms of real wealth that money cannot replace. The point is not to suggest to them that money is meaningless—if I had a bunch of money lying around in my room, I wouldn't hesitate to throw it into my box—but to encourage them to reflect on the deepest sources of personal satisfaction in their lives.

What Makes You the Happiest?

This is a similar question, but it's not the same one. For example, there are three or four books that I especially love, and reread annually. If I lost my copies of those books, I could easily replace the copies, or check out duplicates from the library. But if those books had never been written, my aggregate happiness level would be lower than it currently is.

If I were applying for a mortgage, the enjoyment I take from those books wouldn't persuade a bank official to qualify me for a larger loan. But reading and re-reading those books makes a genuine contribution to my True Net Worth. My life is richer because of them.

I hesitate to speak for my son, but the activity that made him the happiest when he was a young teenager was probably playing his electric guitar. (When he was very young, it was building things with Lego.) The guitar itself could easily have been replaced if something had happened to it, so it couldn't have been considered the most valuable thing he owned. But if he had made a list of the principal sources of happiness in his life at that time, his ability to play his guitar, and the enjoyment he derived from his playing, would probably have been somewhere near the top. At that moment, in other words, guitar-playing was probably one of the most important components of his True Net Worth.

I feel the same way about playing golf. I took up the game ten years ago, on the front steps of middle age, and I've played two or three times a week in decent weather ever since. Most of my closest friends now are guys who I play golf with, and many of my happiest memories over the past decade have arisen from golf-related trips I've taken, or tournaments I've done well in, or silly competitions I've entered with my friends. I've even reconfigured my career, so that today I probably write more about golf than I do about any other subject. Ten years ago, I never thought about golf; now, I think about little else. Golf, in some form, therefore surely belongs near the top of the list in any accounting of my True Net Worth. If I took a higher-paying job that kept me off the golf course during the week, my financial net worth would rise but my True Net Worth would plummet.

Every summer, my family spends a couple of weeks at the same place on Martha's Vineyard. My kids have been going since they were tiny, and they still look forward to going every year. Some of my happiest moments ever have been spent there, and I think both my kids would say the same thing about their own. Our Vineyard vacations don't cost very much and therefore don't have much actual cash value—that is, the money we would save if we stopped going wouldn't add up to a lot, and certainly wouldn't buy much obviously valuable stuff— but those vacations nonetheless make a huge contribution to our True Net Worth. If we could no longer take those vacations (or, worse, if we no longer had our memories of the ones we've already taken), we would be poorer in every sense except the financial one.

Because all such nonfinancial sources of value in life are difficult or impossible to quantify, people tend to ignore them when they make what they (therefore) tend to think of as mainly financial decisions: Should I take on additional responsibilities at work? Should I go back to school? Should I buy a fancier house? All such questions have important financial implications, but their biggest impact on people's lives often has little to do with money. If I moved my family to the West Coast in order to accept a higher-paying job, for example, I would make our usual summer trip to Martha's Vineyard logistically difficult, if not impossible. Would the gain in income make up for the loss in True Net Worth?

On a beautiful autumn weekday a couple of years ago, my friend Bill and I did something we have often done on beautiful autumn weekdays: we knocked off at noon and spent the rest of the day playing golf. Bill is a lawyer, and he knows that he could make more money if he worked for a big firm in a big city instead of a one-lawyer office in a small town, just as I know that I could make more money if I didn't spend so much time hanging around golf clubs with guys like him. On this particular day, we explicitly discussed the bargain we both believed we had struck. "If we worked in New York City," he said, "no amount of money would make it possible for us to leave work at twelve and be on the first tee of any golf course anywhere at twelve-oh-five. We are therefore richer than any golfer in New York, including Donald Trump."

Both of us had arranged our careers to maximize what both of us believed to be a major component of our True Net Worth, even though in doing so we had almost certainly precipitated a significant reduction in our financial net worth. When described in this way, the trade-off may seem obvious, but it seldom seems obvious to people looking at the problem from the opposite direction. Prosperous parents, for example, tend to groom their children to think of life only as a ladder—and don't look down! They unhesitatingly urge their children to reach for the highest possible goals, no matter what the endeavor, but seldom encourage them to think about whether those goals have true value in their lives beyond the difficulty of attaining them. To put it another way, they seldom encourage their children (or themselves) to think carefully and pragmatically about the real sources of their happiness. I often think about a boy who used to attend my children's school. He was a good athlete, and a star on several teams. His parents used to complain constantly to the administration about what they perceived to be the inadequacies of the athletic program, which they felt wasn't worthy of his talents. At last, they pulled him out and sent him to a famous boarding school, where the teams were better—and their son spent the rest of his high-school athletic career sitting on the bench. His parents may have been happier, now that their son was a member of a more glorious team, but the boy's own True Net Worth almost certainly went down.

KEEPING AMBITIONS SEPARATE

When my daughter, at the age of fourteen or fifteen, began to look ahead to college, she decided that she wasn't willing to do the sort of résumé-stuffing that ambitious kids—or, more likely, kids with ambitious parents—often do in high school. The most selective colleges reject so many qualified applicants, she realized, that she might very well end up being turned down regardless of her paper accomplishments. So she decided that, rather than attempting to second-guess an admissions committee, she would live her life the way she wanted to live it and accept the consequences.

As things turned out, she was admitted early to her first choice anyway. But I don't think that was an accident. She was accepted in part, I believe, because her résumé was a genuine reflection of who she is, not because she had somehow managed to fool a committee of strangers into believing she was someone else. I have conducted alumni interviews of college applicants for fifteen years, and I'm pretty sure that I can tell when kids have "interests" that don't really interest them. I feel sorry for those kids, not only because they have cynically wasted hundreds of hours on activities that meant little to them, but also because most of them have been told repeatedly, by their parents and others, that they'll never amount to anything unless they can find ways to fool others into thinking they aren't the people they really are.

John Katzman, who is the founder and chief executive officer of the Princeton Review, a company that coaches students for the SAT and other standardized tests, frequently encounters parents who view their children's lives mainly as extensions of their own ambitions. "You have these parents who are very business- and result-oriented," he told a writer for *New York* magazine in 2001. "In the same way they expect someone who works for them to work all night and close the deal, they approach their kids like a subordinate whose job is to get into Harvard. At any given moment when the kid is doing something off-strategy, like dating, the parent is all over them and saying, 'What haven't you done today to get the Harvard account?'"

Keeping ambitions separate is enormously difficult for some parents. I know a woman who was so obnoxious at her son's soccer games—where she would minutely critique his performance at full volume from the sidelines—that league officials eventually told her she could continue to attend her son's games only if she watched them from inside her car. That worked for a little while. Then she realized that she could honk.

Parents who push their children toward goals that mean nothing to the children—rather than helping their children learn to make thoughtful decisions about how to conduct their own lives both now and in the future—are depriving them of many of life's most important potential sources of happiness and satisfaction. They are squandering their children's True Net Worth.

The True Net Value of Money

I've discussed happiness thus far as though it were free, although of course it's not. In order to leave work for the golf course at noon, my friend Bill and I both needed not only flexible jobs but also enough personal financial resources to cover a half-day vacation in the middle of the week, not to mention paying our membership dues at the club. Arranging our working lives to maximize our True Net Worth, in other words, had required us to earn some decent money as well.

Money is, therefore, an extremely important component of anyone's True Net Worth. But its value is not always self-evident, and it isn't constant. Playing more golf means earning less money, but earning less money makes it harder to pay for more golf. Finding a good balance is a matter of introspection and compromise. My wife and I were tempted once to move to a bigger and fancier house. We could have afforded the change, just barely, but we eventually realized (with the help of our kids) that whatever we might have gained from the change would have been more than offset by what we would have lost. Assuming a big new debt would have meant cutting back everywhere else. Why not take more family vacations instead?

The best way to help our children prepare themselves to wrestle with these issues in their adult lives is to share our own uncertainties and personal discoveries with them in age-appropriate ways. For a long time, we are going to be our children's first and best source of information about what it's really like to live in the adult world. We can help them make better decisions in their own lives if we find ways to let them know—without being defensive or depressing or boastful or frightening—what we think we've gained or lost as a result of the way we've chosen to live.

Very often, such issues are easier to observe dispassionately in the lives of others. If the parent of a friend of your children takes a new job that requires her family to move across the country, you have an opportunity to initiate a potentially illuminating family conversation. You can ask your children how their friends feel about moving, and how they themselves might have felt in the same situation, and what they think it would be like to change schools. All such discussions reinforce the important point that everyone's life is partly a running total of good and bad decisions made in the past, and that existence isn't merely the result of accident, whim, and luck—although, of course, it is also that.

INCREASING TRUE NET WORTH

One useful way to think about True Net Worth is to focus on what I think of as its basic unit of intrinsic value: the hour. I will never have Bill Gates's billions, but there is no reason why I can't enjoy, in any given hour, as much happiness or human fulfillment as he does (or, during the hours when he is being deposed by Justice Department lawyers, considerably more). He has lots more money, but my day and his contain the same number of hours. Even within the confines of my relative poverty, I am fully capable of extracting as much happiness from any of those hours as he is from his.

This is very different from saying that money doesn't

matter. Obviously, money matters very much. But thinking about time rather than money shifts the primary focus away from symbolic assets to real ones. Money that doesn't buy happiness adds nothing to True Net Worth; a contented hour that costs nothing to acquire adds a lot.

The hours in a day conform to all the basic laws of economics, including the ones concerning opportunity cost: an hour you spend on one activity can't also be spent on another. Thinking about True Net Worth encourages you to weigh one hour against another—and maybe even to think of your life as a depreciating asset, which steadily dwindles whether you use it wisely or not.

The Relativity of Wealth

A rich friend of mine once told me, "The secret of happiness is to have poor friends." The profound truth at the heart of his observation is that human beings tend to assess their well-being not by objectively examining their own lives but by comparing their circumstances with those of neighbors, classmates, co-workers, friends, and other people with whom they have regular contact. In most ways, almost all of us enjoy a vastly higher standard of living than even the very richest people who lived just a century or even a half-century ago. (Unlike me, John D. Rockefeller never owned a gigantic color TV or a minivan with a built-in garage-door opener. Ha!) But that thought is little consolation if your best friend's kitchen has three sinks and yours has only two.

Given the overall condition of the human race during most of the history of the civilized world, you would think that simply not having bubonic plague would be enough to put most of us in cheerful moods—but, no, we want a hot tub, too. As the centuries go by, people simply find different reasons to feel grumpy. Every improvement in one's situation is negated by an equal or greater improvement in someone else's. The fact that I, unlike Alexander the Great, have indoor plumbing doesn't keep me from feeling shabby when I consider the wealth of my wealthy friends.

Kids are capable of going both ways on this emotionally fraught issue. That is, they can sometimes be delightfully oblivious of even huge disparities in the material circumstances of their friends, yet they can also sometimes be crueler and more appallingly hung up about minor differences than even the most appalling adults. No matter where your family falls on the continuum of prosperity in comparison with your acquaintances, you can do your kids a favor by helping them find ways to be comfortable with who they are yet encouraging them to be sensitive to the feelings of others.

The only good advice I've ever given my kids in this regard was a suggestion I made concerning how to treat wealthier friends who were constantly boasting about their wealth: when a rich friend brags in some money-related way (about a father's new car that cost "a million dollars," for example), don't be drawn into an argument ("That's impossible!")—just pretend to be blown away ("Wow! That's really cool!"). This always works, even with grown-ups. People who boast about possessions usually do so out of a feeling of insecurity, which argument only aggravates.

AN EXERCISE: MAPPING TRUE NET WORTH

Almost two decades ago, a short-lived magazine called *Wigwag* invited one contributor each month to draw a map of his or her life—a map in which geographic and topographical features represented major turning points, sources of happiness, fields of interest, and so on. I think drawing a map of one's life is a good way to think about True Net Worth, and I think this is an especially good exercise to try with young kids. Someday when everyone is bored, ask your kids to try to represent their life as a map. You might ask them what the tallest mountain would be on a map of their life. And whether there would be more than one country. And what the oceans would be called. Where is school? Where is your family? What would your summer vacations look like if you drew them on a map?

Of course, you should sit down with them and draw a map of your own life, too.

8

THE BEST INVESTMENT YOU CAN MAKE FOR YOUR CHILDREN

THOUGHTFUL PARENTS OFTEN FRET about how best to invest for their children's futures. Zero-coupon treasuries maturing the year they leave for college? Roth IRAs filled with tech stocks and junk bonds? Gold ingots stored in abandoned fallout shelters? Real estate investment trusts?

Here's my best advice: Read to them even more than you already do.

That's it, the best investment you can make for your kids. If your children are still young enough to tolerate close personal contact with you, there's little you can do for them that will produce bigger long-term and short-term profits, both for them and for you. Even better, reading to children is also a good example of the best sort of family activity: quality time that is also quantity time.

Children who are read to regularly from early ages develop lifelong skills that can't be acquired from a DVD player or the Disney Channel. They become better listeners and find it easier to pay attention in school. Their vocabularies grow rapidly, and grammar seems less mysterious to them. They don't immediately lose interest in any idea that is harder to grasp than a television commercial. They develop the patience to follow a complex problem to its solution. They become better writers all by themselves, through their ample powers of imitation.

Reading to children helps them become avid readers, and avid readers have lifelong advantages that can't be bought for cash. Good readers do better in school, score higher on standardized tests (including standardized math tests, which, after all, consist mainly of words), attend better colleges, hold more interesting jobs, write more persuasive legal briefs, make better conversation, and become less and less likely to gripe about being bored. And they're easier to raise and more fun to hang around with.

Most important of all, children who grow up immersed in books develop the ability to answer their own questions. If they suddenly become interested in doctors, insects, babies, the solar system, earthquakes, or fire engines, they know how to pursue the subject until their curiosity has been satisfied. Gradually, they acquire a skill shared by the greatest scholars in the world: the ability to educate themselves. Later in life, they will be able to use that same ability to teach themselves about the bond market.

All of these steadily evolving skills have economic value in adult life. Highly literate workers have immense competitive advantages throughout the economy. Employees who know how to write compelling memos are more likely to get what they want than employees who don't. Stock analysts who are comfortable readers don't get lost in fine print. Turning your children into good readers will give them an edge they will keep for the rest of their lives.

THERE'S A SELFISH ANGLE, TOO!

Raising good readers has important advantages for parents as well. Children who learn to love books at an early age become increasingly adept at amusing themselves as they grow older, leaving their parents with more time for themselves. Both of our kids pretended to read long before they could really do it. We would overhear them entertaining a stuffed animal or a doll, often with an improved version of a story we had read to them earlier. (When our daughter was little, I heard her pretending to read the Christmas story, using her copy of *Beezus and Ramona* as her Bible, in which Jesus had "long pants, a royal coat, shoes made of wood, and long, straight socks.") They could occupy themselves during plane trips, long car rides, and frantic afternoons. Both of them slipped easily into real reading without knowing how they had done it. They seemed to learn almost by osmosis. A few weeks after my daughter discovered that she could read—while thumbing through a story book at the library shortly before she turned five—I found her in our living room happily reading *Little House on the Prairie* to herself.

In families with preschool-age children, books can help to keep the peace. A two-year-old who is cranky, bored, and angry at the world can often be transformed back into an angel by a parent with a pile of library books. Sometimes the change is instantaneous: book opens, crying stops, thumb pops into mouth. Reading to children is good for parents, too. You get to spend a quiet half-hour snuggled up on the couch with someone who loves you, and you become conversant with the names and distinguishing characteristics of many species of dinosaurs. Rainy days become less of a problem, because you and your child can always kill a desperate hour by going to the library—a trip with a double payoff, because it leaves you both with something to look forward to when you get back home. (Besides, wouldn't you rather read aloud than spend an hour drinking tea from empty doll cups or pretending to be Batman?)

Books can transform the long, hectic stretch between dinner and bedtime into a pleasure instead of an ordeal. Even very tired children are often too wound up in the evening to be simply thrown into their beds. Story time provides a gentle transition from the chaos of the day to that blissful moment when the household's youngest members have all dropped off to sleep. Books help everyone cool down.

MORE BENEFITS FOR PARENTS

One of the great benefits of reading to children is that it gives parents an opportunity to re-experience favorite books from their own childhoods, or to discover great books that they missed the first time around. My favorite reading when I was in fifth and sixth grades was J. R. R. Tolkien's Middle Earth trilogy, *The Lord of the Rings.* As much as I loved those books when I was a kid, I would have been highly unlikely to read them again as an adult, if I hadn't thought of reading them to my son (first when he was six or seven, and again when he was eleven). Helping your children become good readers can reawaken your own interest in good books. It can improve your sense of well-being, and give you an increased sense of control over your hectic life.

Once children have begun to read on their own, the benefits for parents multiply. Good readers are harder to bore and therefore less needy of parental intervention. They're fun to be with. They're interesting to talk to. They're easy to travel with. They keep up with the news. And they share a major cultural legacy with their parents.

INVESTING IN READING

The best time to introduce a child to books is long before the child is able to read. Babies enjoy looking at pictures and being read to. My son's first real smile was prompted by a picture book containing a photograph of a crying baby—proof that reveling in the misfortunes of others is an inborn human trait. Parents sometimes feel silly reading stories to children who can't talk, but children like it, and they learn to like it more the more you do it. They like the pictures, they like being held, they like the attention, they like the sound of your voice. Children who are read to from very early ages don't need to be taught later that books can be sources of comfort, entertainment, and learning.

Reading to preschool children requires a fairly high level of determination by parents. Two or three twenty-four-page picture books don't last very long—even if you read each one over and over, as young children often demand. Raising good readers requires parents to keep the household well supplied with interesting books, and that means frequent trips to the library.

Many libraries don't limit the number of children's books that you can check out. We used to visit half a dozen libraries in rotation, and lug our books around in big canvas bags. When our kids were in preschool, visits from us were dreaded by some local librarians, who would scurry off to re-alphabetize the card catalog when they saw us trudging toward the checkout counter with our bags. Other parents waiting in line would often ask, "Are you teachers?" as though no other explanation were conceivable. We viewed late fines and lost fees as an unavoidable cost of doing business.

Trips to the library were eagerly anticipated in our family. The kids especially liked having the opportunity to discover a good author or series or category that they hadn't previously exhausted. When our daughter, at the age of six or so, suddenly became interested in medicine, our local librarian surprised her by ordering an entire series of books about kids with terrible illnesses. (At around that time, our daughter invented a guessing game in which one player would pretend to be an interesting disease and the other players would try to guess its identity by asking questions: Are you primarily a disease of adults? Are you caused by a virus? Are you invariably fatal?) We sometimes grabbed dinner at a fast-food restaurant on the way home, and when we went in to eat, the new books came with us.

When we traveled by plane with our kids, our carry-on luggage consisted almost entirely of library books. When we traveled by car, book bags filled the empty seats. One of the great breakthroughs in our family's travel history occurred on a trip during which our daughter first entertained both herself and her young brother by reading to him for long stretches at a time, keeping both of them happily and productively occupied for mile after mile after mile. My wife and I looked at each other in wonder and tried not to break the mood.

HOW TO READ TO A KID

Children sometimes have trouble sitting still for story time, but that doesn't always mean they're not interested in what you're reading. Young children can often listen better if they're doing something with their hands: building a sofa-cushion fortress, dressing a doll, playing checkers with a sibling, taking a bath, even looking at or reading a different book. Parents sometimes become discouraged and stop reading aloud when their kids hop up from the couch, but they shouldn't. Kids just need to wiggle more than grown-ups do.

Kids may also have reading tastes that, to adults, seem discouraging. When my son was very little, he loved a picture book about a boy eating spaghetti in a restaurant. My wife and I would read the book over and over, at his request, and he would sometimes ask us to begin again when we were little more than halfway through. For unknowable reasons, the restaurant book made a huge impression on him. I hated thinking that a book about eating spaghetti could be more appealing than, say, a beautifully illustrated story about Ellis Island which had been chosen by librarians as one of the best children's books of the year. But kids like what they like. If you want books to be essential to their lives, you have to let them follow their interests (even as you surreptitiously attempt to shape them).

READING TO OLDER CHILDREN

Reading aloud to children should continue for as long as possible after the children have begun to read on their own. In fact, reading to new readers may be the best way to reinforce their developing skills. It also exposes children to good books that would be too challenging for them to tackle on their own. A first-grader who needs help sounding out *The Cat in the Hat* may nonetheless enjoy listening to *Tom Sawyer* or *A Wrinkle in Time* or *The Chronicles of Narnia*—sophisticated books that he or she might not be ready to tackle alone for years.

Parents shouldn't force hard books on young children, but few kids' taste in literature conforms exactly with publishers' age recommendations. If you read regularly to your kids, their growing literary sophistication will surprise you again and again. Desperate for something to read to my son one day when he was four or five, I grabbed *Treasure Island* off the shelf and was astonished to discover that, despite the archaic language and sometimes confusing action, we both were captivated right to the end.

Once children reach junior high school or even late elementary school, they will probably resist being read to. ("Stop using so much expression," a ninth grader I know sneered at his mother, who was reading to a younger sibling.) But that doesn't mean reading should cease to be a family activity. Here are some ideas about how to keep reading a part of family life even after the children are old enough to be embarrassed by their parents:

- Older kids in a family can often be pressed into service—or even paid, if that seems appropriate—to read to younger siblings. If so, they will discover what parents inevitably discover, or rediscover, when they read aloud to their kids: a lot of children's books are really good. (Incidentally, if you have children who baby-sit, you should encourage them to take good read-aloud books with them when they work. They'll be more popular, with both parents and kids, and their young charges will be better behaved.)

- Older children who would rather be scalded and skinned than be read to by a parent may enjoy listening to recorded books. You can play recorded books during long drives in the car, for half an hour every evening, at breakfast before school, or at other times. Most libraries now offer (or are able to obtain) a broad selection of recorded books, and a growing number of titles can be downloaded from the Internet and played back on MP3 players. Even reluctant readers can be swept up in a good story if they don't have to do their own page-turning. Later, they may feel inspired to seek out printed books on their own. (Try starting with a good mystery.

Your audience will probably stick around long
enough to find out who done it.)

- A sickbed is a good place to introduce an older
child to recorded books: kids with fevers can't
get up and walk away, and even reluctant readers
may come to prefer a good recorded book to
daytime TV. Other good times for listening to
books: while cooking, drawing, building a
model, tying flies, cleaning a room, working out
on an exercise machine, driving to school.

- If you don't make a big deal out of it, older children will sometimes eavesdrop while you read
to younger children. Position yourself strategi-
cally during story time, and choose your reading
material wisely, and you may attract a wider
audience.

- The next time you and your kids go shopping,
stop at the bookstore and treat each child to a
paperback book of his or her choosing. You'll
spend about the same as you would for ice
cream. And books don't melt.

- Read at the dinner table a few times a week. Sit-
down family meals are said to be disappearing in
America, but if you still have them, you might
consider occasionally making them a time for

enjoying books or magazines. (Your kids aren't
going to tell you what they did at school anyway,
so you won't miss much in the way of conversation.) I once bought a dozen leather-covered paperweights, which I kept in a bowl on our
kitchen table. With two weights holding down
the edges of whatever book I was reading at dinner, I could keep both hands free for eating. My
weights never caught on with the other members of my family, though, so I moved most of
them to my office, where I use them to hold
down the piles of junk on my desk.

- If reading on the road doesn't make your kids
  feel ill, encourage them to stock your car with
  books. More and more parents nowadays spend
  huge blocks of time transporting their kids
  between school, soccer practice, dance lessons,
  friends' houses, and the mall. Most kids spend
  that driving time staring out the window, com-
  plaining, listening to music, or pestering each
  other. Books can help. At our house, the last
  thing we say before we head out to the garage is,
  "Does everyone have something to read?"
  (Except the driver, obviously.)

- Reading silently in the same room with an older
  child is a pleasant, low-risk way to spend time

together. You aren't talking, so you are in no danger of fighting about friends, grades, hair, clothes, table manners, or any other loaded family issue. You and your child can lose yourselves in your books without losing touch. And if you occasionally find a single book that interests both of you, you can share an experience without getting all gross about it.

LONG TERM VS. SHORT TERM

Goals that are important to you may seem less so to your kids. Parents tend to focus on the long term—college, jobs, saving for retirement—while kids are interested in the here and now. Harping on the long-range benefits of education may turn off rather than inspire a reluctant reader; warning a fifth-grader that she'll never get into Yale if she doesn't turn off that TV is unlikely to have the intended effect. The best way to encourage reading and writing skills is to emphasize short-term rewards: a good laugh, an interesting afternoon, a less boring car ride.

Television, for all of its considerable rewards and pleasures, is the enemy. Living entirely without television would be virtually impossible in our society, but we should all make an effort to restrict access to TV and video games during certain times of every day, forcing our children (and ourselves) to seek alternatives. Television programs we watch are an indisputably important part of our culture—for years, my family has planned mealtimes around *The Simpsons*—but all of us would be smarter and more interesting if we watched less TV. The trick is to reduce everyone's reliance on the boob tube without making *Beavis and Butthead* seem irresistibly attractive. And no one should try to give up television cold turkey.

As with many other kinds of behavior, it's the parents who set the most important example. Parents who read tend to have children who read. Parents with strong vocabularies tend to have children with strong vocabularies. If you want books to be a part of your children's lives, you need to be sure that books are a part of your life, too.

TASTE IN BOOKS

Parents often try to prevent their children from reading "trash"—comic books, teen magazines, joke books, unsophisticated science fiction. But no one can live by classics alone, least of all kids.

Beginning readers need to build their confidence

(and stretch their imagination) with reading materials that don't overwhelm them. There's nothing wrong with that. Many good adult readers and writers spent their childhoods buried in comic books. Parents should be aware of what their children are reading, but they shouldn't be quick to step in with restrictions and prohibitions. Kids will revert to television if books are made to seem too much like medicine. Most readers, when left on their own, eventually find their way to books that are worthy of them. (Besides, when was the last time you curled up with the poems of John Milton or any of the other classics you read in college? As the poet John Berryman once said, Thank God for second-rate books, or else what would anyone read after the age of twenty-one?)

Being lenient about what constitutes acceptable reading matter can also be the key to catching the interest of a reluctant reader. A child who loves motorcycles and hates books may nonetheless devour a motorcycle magazine—if the magazine is made available, and if studying it is treated by you as a laudable activity. If you follow your children's passions of the moment, you can sometimes lure them into good books by way of the back door. For more than a few well-educated adults, the journey to the world of literature began with *Mad* magazine.

How to Begin

As with all long-term investments, the most effective strategy may require time travel. If your kids are ten or eleven years old and you suddenly march into their room with your reading glasses and an armload of library books, they're going to give you a look you won't soon forget. But if they resist, you can always read more to yourself. And you can look forward to reading to your grandchildren.

If your children are still young and impressionable, all you have to do is begin. If you already read to your kids before bed, you can simply add other story times, at other crucial times of the day—ideally, perhaps, at times when they might otherwise be watching TV. Or take them to the library this weekend and load up on books. Best of all: the potential payoff, though huge, is entirely tax-free.

9

THE ULTIMATE PAYOFF

MY FATHER UNDERWENT A BIG OPERATION several years ago, when he was seventy-six. The surgery lasted for six hours, and he ended up with sixty-one staples in his abdomen. He didn't recover from the anesthesia for a couple of days, and when he began to regain consciousness, the doctors had to put restraints on his arms, to keep him from ripping out various tubes and catheters and monitoring devices. He was on a ventilator for a while, too. It was a rough time for him, and an even rougher one for my mom, who, after all, was conscious through the whole thing. She was at his side when he opened his eyes. The first thing he said, in a voice that was weak but filled with hope, was "Am I at the country club?"—exactly the question that I myself would have asked in the same situation.

My dad had retired nearly twenty years before, after a thirty-year career as a stockbroker at a regional investment firm in the Midwest. Shortly after his retirement, he turned over the bulk of his savings to a professional money manager, because he felt that he no longer had a close enough connection to the financial world to do a decent job himself. He was never satisfied with the professional's results, however; the pro's investments never seemed to work out as well as the ones my father made on his own, in a separate portfolio over which he had retained personal control, mostly just to amuse himself. After a couple of years, at the urging of various family members, he got rid of the expert and went back to handling things himself.

I was delighted by that decision. As a teenager I had spent two summers working as gopher at his firm, and, once I got the hang of the job—on my first day, I left a fifty-thousand-dollar check lying on the cold marble floor of the First National Bank of Kansas City—there were many occasions on which I felt proud of how highly the other brokers regarded him. He was one of the most successful salesmen in the firm, and he achieved his success without churning accounts or pushing foolish investments on ignorant people or doing any of the other unscrupulous things that successful brokers often do. He was honest and careful, and he made a lot of money for a lot of people. He also taught me, both directly and indirectly, how to be a reasonably competent manager of my own financial resources.

For more than twenty years, my father was my main fiscal sounding board. He helped me think my way through all the main financial checkpoints of my life, from quitting my first job to buying my first house to saving for my children's education to planning for my retirement. He taught me to take a long-term view of the economy in general while never allowing myself to become complacent about investment decisions I had made in the past. Most of all, he inspired me to emulate his patient, rational example. On more than a few occasions when I was in a panic about some recent economic cataclysm, I would call him on the phone and he would talk me back to rationality—not telling me what to do, but calmly helping me regain my intellectual bearings.

AFTER THE OPERATION

During the weeks and months following his big operation, my dad made a remarkable recovery. But we quickly realized that he had nonetheless suffered a significant setback, and that he was unlikely ever to be able to resume the role he had once played so ably as the manager of his and my mother's investments. We also discovered, after examining some of his financial records, that the ideal moment for him to give up that role had probably passed some months before. My mother, my siblings, and I decided that we had to intervene. But what would Dad's reaction be? And what would we ourselves do if he didn't agree?

I went to talk to him in his room at the nursing home where he was recuperating. I said, "Dad, what would you say if I told you I had an older friend who needed to support himself and his wife on their savings for the rest of their lives, and that he wanted you to manage those savings for him."

"I'd say you were crazy," my father said.

"Well," I said, "that friend is you, and I think you're right."

He laughed. I explained why I thought we needed to step in, and I said that the main reason I felt confident in doing so was that I was pretty sure I was doing exactly what he would have done in the same situation, had the roles been reversed. I told him that everything I knew about money I had learned from him, and that I now intended to apply that knowledge in the way I believed he had prepared me to apply it. We discussed investing principles in general for a few minutes. Then he said, "What you say doesn't offend me. Do it."

So I did. The experience was mildly traumatic for my

mom, my siblings, and me—a couple of nights later, my mom woke up in a panic, having just dreamt that my father had come back from the nursing home and angrily demanded, "What have you done with my stocks?"—but it wasn't at all traumatic for my dad. A few days after our big discussion, he told my mom, "Dave said I wasn't going to like what he had to tell me. But I did like it, because now I don't have to worry about it anymore."

I'm not 100 percent certain that the steps we took were the best steps we possibly could have taken. But I am absolutely confident that our unanimity and the courage we needed to proceed came from my dad himself. He had never been sentimental about money management; he believed in results. When the time came, we were able to act because he had prepared us to act fearlessly in his behalf.

And there, if you need one, is an elegantly selfish reason for helping your kids learn to feel comfortable with money. We are our children's financial guardians today, but they will be our financial guardians tomorrow, assuming that we are sufficiently lucky to live long enough to need their help. We therefore have a direct, personal, long-term interest in doing everything we can to prepare them for the moment when our actions will compel them to shoulder our problems for us. The better we teach them now, the better they'll do when circumstances force them to take control.

Everyone knows stories of families that have been torn apart by the complicated emotions that arise when accumulated wealth passes from one generation to the next. (Re-read *King Lear* if you don't believe me.) I know of an affluent family that for more than a year has been locked in bitter litigation over the wording of wills—children against parents, siblings against siblings— and no one in that family has even died yet. Lawsuits like that tear families apart, and the damage can endure for generations. What sort of legacy is that? Is the purpose of building a family fortune merely to facilitate the destruction of the family from within?

The better we teach our children now, the more likely they'll be to do a good job when the time comes for them to gently lift our hands from the steering wheel. That's the potential payback, if you feel you need one. Do your best to help your kids today; someday, your own security and happiness may depend on their ability to return the favor.

About the Author

David Owen is a staff writer for *The New Yorker* and a contributing editor of *Golf Digest,* for which he writes a monthly humor column. The author of thirteen previous books, he lives with his family in northwest Connecticut.